Magic Realized

And Other Poems on the Human Spirit

CONSTRUCTED OF MAGIC
VOLUME TWO

Louis Alan Swartz

Illustrations by Diane Woods

HUGO HOUSE PUBLISHERS, LTD.

Constructed of Magic and other Poems on the Immortality of the Human Spirit.
VOLUME 2

Magic Realized and Other Poems on the Human Spirit

ISBN: 978-1-936449-46-0

Illustrations: Diane Woods, www.dianewoodsdesign.com

Cover Design & Interior Layout: Ronda Taylor, www.rondataylor.com

Hugo House Publishers, Ltd.

Denver, Colorado
Austin, Texas
www.HugoHousePublishers.com

Dedication

To L. Ron Hubbard

Contents

{ 1 } Love and Marriage

{ 2 } Children

{ 3 } Grandmothers, Grandfathers, Mothers and Fathers

{ 4 } Human Sanctity

{ 5 } Aesthetics

{ 6 } Ideas, Images, and Places

{ 7 } Death, the Spirit, and Immortality

Foreword

There's powerful magic in Louis' poetry. I'm one of the most optimistic people I know, but even I see daily living can batter our spirits and drain some of the magic out of our lives.

That's where Louis comes in.

Louis' beautiful poetry replenishes your soul. "Replenish" means to fill up again, from the Latin *re-* again and *plenus*—complete, fullness. It has the same root as the word "plenty" which means "abundance, profusion."

This poetry will inspire a powerful belief in yourself and restore the beauty of the world around you. It will fill you with potent confidence that anything (and everything) is possible.

One of my closest friends for the past 30 years is a gifted painter. She's one of the most young-at-heart people I've ever known. I don't think she'll mind if I tell you how old she is—she's 70. She'd been living on her own for many years when she read the first volume of Louis' poetry, *Constructed of Magic*.

She wrote to Louis to tell him how deeply his poetry moved her. Soon after, Louis asked Diane to illustrate a special issue of his love poetry to be published for Valentine's Day. Diane sent him five paintings to choose for his book cover. Louis selected one and asked her to send it to his publisher.

Diane accidentally sent the publisher all five paintings ... and the publisher fell in love with her. George set surprised eyes on the paintings and knew all he needed to know, all that was important, about Diane. And he knew he loved her.

I still laugh about the next conversation I had with Diane. She and George hadn't talked yet and she was wondering why the publisher's emails to her seemed so unusually … she struggled for the right word … so unusually *warm* for someone she didn't know.

During these early emails with George, Diane discovered that she could fully be herself without any restraints, that it was wonderful to share her innermost ideas and beliefs with this man, that he deeply understood her, that he was a man she admired. Diane fell equally in love.

They carried on a gorgeous correspondence via email and then had their first phone call …. which led to their first (nervous and fabulous) meeting in person … which led to blissfully accepting George's heartfelt proposal of marriage and Diane's moving to Austin, Texas to make a home with George. The most recent email I received from Diane she wrote, "We belong together."

A love of Louis' poetry brought them together and, as a result, the book you're now holding has been illustrated and published by these two rejoicing, exuberant 70-year old kids who, inspired by this poetry, found love and adore each other.

Louis' poetry is much more than just for lovers. I can give you countless other examples of the powerful magic of Louis' poems.

Reading his poetry healed a severe 49-year upset between a brother and sister.

A pain-filled grieving young girl was able to come to terms with the loss of her mother, giving her a much needed sense of peace.

A career woman experienced a profound spiritual re-awakening as she recognized the divine within herself.

A successful businessman found a way to express tenderness to his wife of many years and restore joy to his marriage.

A minister wrapped powerful Sunday sermons around the poems, uplifting the congregation with grace and the optimism born of the immortality of the human spirit.

An artist unleashed boundless suppressed artistic talent and is now joyously painting and selling art at a mad rate.

Many men (ones who typically don't read poetry) have expressed that reading Louis' poetry took the blocks off of their emotions and made them feel again. I could go on ….

The purpose of these poems is to restore the magic in yourself and the world around you, to unleash the impeccable beauty, grandeur and unlimited potential of your spirit. To help you spread your wings and fly.

Plunge into this book and find the poems that sail straight to your heart. There's a miracle in these pages waiting for you.

You'll be replenished with that magic elixir of hope, self-belief, love and courage that makes you remember you can move mountains … makes you a better lover, warrior, person … nourishes your life force and your very soul. You'll feel complete again. Very likely you'll feel ridiculously happy.

Turn the page and let the magic begin …

Ingrid Gudenas, Educator and Coach

Introduction

I believe in magic. I believe in magic in little ways and in huge ways. It is my viewpoint that our task here on earth is restoration. To me, the finest and most crucial magic is the magic of helping to restore you to the full magnitude of your individual greatness.

It is a matter of great concern for me how deeply my fellowman has appeared to have lost his self-respect. But when you look at the tattered track of this universe it is understandable. The reason I write and the reason I live is to help you restore your self-respect—your belief in yourself. It is my purpose to assist you to gain touch with your personal, unique aesthetic* and with the vast abilities you possess as an immortal spiritual being.

Aesthetic - relating to pure beauty rather than to other considerations.
Collins English Dictionary Online

Note on Definitions:

I have provided definitions of words at the end of some poems. Words often have more than one meaning. My intention was to ensure that the meaning with which I was using the word was clearly understood.

Magic Realized

I can see the predawn glow

Emerging in indigo skies.

There's a future filled with hope

In your newly opened eyes.

Sailing ships wait

In the harbor below.

There is some place

Special we wish to go.

The sun is rising

In indigo skies.

Magic recognized.

Magic realized.

{ 1 }

Love and Marriage

~⌒~

I intend to make you ridiculously happy.

~⌒~

The Fine Sensitivities of Loving

The fine sensitivities of loving:
Scarcely voiced crucial communications,
The joy real understanding can bring,
Fulfillment of finest expectations,
The pleasure of spending a day with you,
On fire as we exchange points of view.

First

First breath,
        word,
             step.
First snow, first birthday,
First rocking horse.

My very first suit,
Tweed with short pants.

The first day of school,
Learning to read,
Learning to write.

First roller skates,
Out of control
On the hills nearby.

My cherished
Wooden wagon
Delivering papers
House to house.

First dog lost
Running before
The street car.
First car, date,
Romance, love
And loss,

First time she let me
Carry her books
And walk her
Home from school.

(It was then I
achieved immortality.)

Someone Fell in Love Last Night

I believe someone fell in love last night
In the alcove just outside my door.
Love's initial exploration had no other place to go.
I heard the muted giggles of romance,
A heady mix of silliness and passion,
Music of new love's first infusion.*
They're trying to be quiet so no one can hear.
The added thrill someone might be listening.
I lay still in quiet awe of the awkward incubation.*
Whispered words sanctified the cramped hallway
And in the giddy wee hours of the morning
A young lady and a young man fell in love last night.

Infusion—infuse—to fill or cause to be filled with something
Infusion—the act or process of infusing
American Heritage Dictionary
Incubation—incubate—to cause to develop or take form
Webster's New World College Dictionary

Gold Filigree Earrings

Take off your earrings,
Gold filigree,
Laced with amethyst,
Sapphire and jade,
Wondrous in themselves.

Take them off.
Take off your
Golden rings and
Lay them on
The table.

Take a deep breath.
You are here with me.
You have no place to be.
No one is expecting you.
You have no quota tonight.
You are just here with me
And a thousand
Years of eternity.

Riding East from Chicago to D.C.

Riding the train
From Chicago to D.C.
An aching loss
Wouldn't let go of me.
Stars in Midwest sky.
What actually happens
When people die?

Crossing the Midwest plain,
Will I ever
See her again?
Certain I'd know her
By any name.

Quiet towns
Bedded down for the night.
What happened to her
Doesn't seem right.
Dealing with unlimited grief.
A long train ride,
Hoping for some relief.

Meanwhile in the next car,
A woman, frail and delicate,
Jerked up from her seat,
Restless and disconsolate.*
A mortal hurt lodged inside,
Would do anything to ameliorate.*

"If I could I would
This heart amputate."
New found horror of life
Utterly unable to assimilate.
An overwhelming desire
To be able to communicate.

"Overcome by desolation,
Isolation of my own creation,
Desperate need for someone to talk to.
Prowled the train like a hungry wolf
And wound up sitting next to you."

She told me of her Chicago loss
And the rivers of sadness
She was required to cross.

Louis A. Swartz

Retaining her integrity
At massive spiritual cost.

Felt emotion I thought
Had been utterly lost,
Listening beyond listening.
In the Midwest dawn
The solitary train travelled on.

Story of a life upheaval,
The consuming devastation
Caused by pure evil.
"Unable to imagine
How on earth I could ever
Love someone again."

"Then was ugly, but then was then,"
I said, as I held her
Tiny body trembling,
Tears welling in her eyes,
Warm sun rising
In Midwest skies.

"Perhaps there's something to learn,
Perhaps there's something to realize."
She took a deep breath
As she dried her eyes.

Death of a child,
Death of a dream,
Death of a world
That was never as it seemed.

We sat together
In the rising dawn.
Beyond the train window
Passing farm after farm.

Sleepy towns
Listening
To lovely train sounds.
Communication
Of living souls,
Awakened dreams,
Rekindled goals.

Gracious lady,
Half an angel,
Half an elf,
Falling in love
In spite of myself.

She asked me intensely
"Is there any life at all
Beyond this utter insanity?"
"That question gives me
An enormous responsibility.
Consider creating
Something with me."

"I appreciate how you've
Listened to me."
Tentatively, tremulously,*
Hesitatingly,
"I'm willing to see
If possibly I could
Create something with thee."
As the train traveled on
In the beautiful breaking
Midwest Dawn.

*Disconsolate—so unhappy that nothing will comfort (Webster's New World College Dictionary)
*Ameliorate—to make better; improve (Macmillan Dictionary for Students)
*Tremulously—timid or fearful (American Heritage Dictionary)

Love Note

In the fridge I left you spicy chili
Made from your grandma's recipe.
Please don't you wait up for me.
You make me intensely happy.
With you I feel limitlessly free.
In the kettle on the stove is *chai* tea.
I so appreciate your respect for me
And the things you've helped me to see.
There are lovely apricots fresh from tree.
I love you from now to infinity.

He Loves

There were flowers beside the path
Of deep purple, lavender and orange.
He saw them and they caused him happiness.
He loves.

There was the night sky,
Viewing it from the high country.
Clarity of the evening stars.
It causes him to feel awe.
He loves.

Early morning children off to school
With their book bags and lunch boxes,
Scrubbed faces and fun filled hearts.
He watches them board.
He loves.

Through a window high above the street
Sound of French horn, band practice,
Triumphal passage of sound.
He listens.
He loves.

At the market melons piled high.
Sweet smell of the spice sellers stand
Tended by a child with a summer face.
He sees and he smells.
He loves.

Louis A. Swartz

Early morning breakfast table is set just so,
Freshly gathered wild flowers in the center,
White linen table cloth embroidered with reds.
Tea kettle steaming, eggs cooking, bread warming.
He sees. He smells.
He loves.

Dawn light breaking through kitchen window.
Cozy cat sleeps comfortably in the corner.
Morning paper lands with a plop on the porch.
He sees. He feels.
He loves.

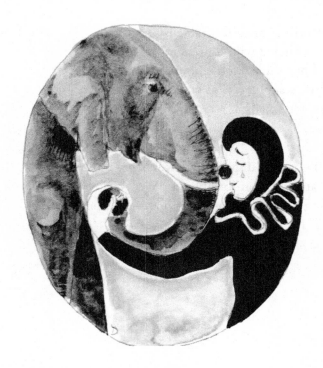

The Elephant Man and the Sad Faced Clown

I cared for the elephants at the circus.
I watered them and fed them.
I washed them down with a big scrubber
And cleaned and trimmed their feet.

I learned to speak to the elephants
And was able to gain their trust
And taught them many tricks
Which we performed under the big top.

I would know when they felt pain
And when they were expressing love.
I felt much more comfortable with them
Than with the human beings.

Once when I was very ill,
They gathered around my trailer
And refused to leave until I
Came out healthy again.

They were kind in the extreme.
They had an uncanny ability
To perceive my feelings
And respond appropriately.

So it was when the Sad Faced Clown
Came to work for the Circus.
I didn't know where she came from.
She just kind of showed up one day.

When I saw her for the first time
She was speaking to Hercules,
A wonderful young elephant.
I let her alone with him.

She was wearing her sad face,
A red bulb on the end of her nose
And heart wrenching tears
Painted on her cheeks.

She left the elephants
And went to perform.
I followed her
To see her act.

She communicated
A sadness of nearly
Incomprehensible
Magnitude.

The sadness
Was accompanied

By a compassion
And a hope.

Laced into the loss
Was somehow the joy
Of living beyond tragedy
And catastrophe.

 All was said
With her hands and face.
There was a humanity
That came through.

And a tenderness,
Humility, love
And benevolence
In spite of all suffered.

The men and women
In the audience
Openly cried
Without restraint.

But they cried
More for the hope
And humanity
Than the sadness.

It was a releasing
Of impacted* emotion
Accumulated
Over centuries.

In some way I knew
She had personally
Experienced
These feelings.

Louis A. Swartz

She continued to come
To visit the elephants
In the morning each day
And to speak to them.

Many weeks passed
And then months.
She continued to come
But we never spoke.

I left her apples for them.
She fed them with gusto
Laughing with the elephants
Running up and down.

As time progressed
There was a warmth
That began to grow
Strongly between us.

I, more and more,
Anticipated her arrival
Each early morning when
The elephants greeted her.

When she was there
A calmness would pervade*
Among the elephants,
A peace would prevail.

They would do something
With the tiny clown
Only describable
As inaudible purring.

Sometimes they'd gently
Lift her with their trunks

{ 15 }

And pass her
One to the next.

One day, a year after she came,
I was cleaning Hercules' feet.
She came up to me and watched
For what seemed a long time.

Then for the very first time
She spoke in a gentle voice,
"Can I be your friend?"
"Of course," I told her.
That was all we said.

She still comes each day.
All that has changed is
She always smiles at me.

She exudes a kindness
And respect unlike
Anything I have ever
Experienced.

I don't know where this will go.
I would be happy to have it
Remain just as it is with the Sad
Faced Clown coming each day.

The warmth continues to grow,
Combined with mutual delight.
The elephants quietly watch,
Knowing something we don't know.

*Impacted—pressed tightly together; driven firmly in; wedged in
Webster's New World College Dictionary
*Pervade— To be present throughout
American Heritage Dictionary

Early Morning Note

Your morning vitamins are
 In a cup on the nightstand.
Cereal with fresh blueberries
Is on the kitchen counter.
I wakened early for a long walk
At dawn along the ocean.
Somehow I've lost track.
I laid out clean clothes for you.
You'll be ok without me.
I need some time to myself
To rearrange my dreams.
Somehow we should have
Been further along by now.
I want you to know I love you,
But what does that really mean?
Help Frank get up and to school.
Late summer I always get so lonely.
I should've stayed with the theater.
I don't blame you for anything.
I'll walk with the moist sea wind
In my face listening to sea sounds,
Watching the sea birds flying.
I'll walk to the lighthouse and home.
I think we can make a go of this.
I will do my very best to put it right.

Note on Refrigerator Door

On the third shelf, behind
Yesterday's stew,
Are fresh and lovely strawberries
I left for you.
I never intended to leave
In such a graceless way.
Never wanted to worry you
Or spoil your special Sunday.

In a carved wooden box
Near the back, under
Your underwear and socks
Is the marvelous ring
You gave me so earnestly.
This I could not bring.

Can't tell you where
To forward my mail.
For now, just keep it there.
With my scattered mind
I'm certain I left something behind.
I know how much I'll miss you.
Save me a little of that stew.

⌒

Reconciliation

There was an oblique* kindness
In her unlovely prose,
Almost as an afterthought
But at the same time
Deeply felt.

Louis A. Swartz

Buried in the e-mail,
Opaque* and twisted,
Was a confused desire
To put it right again.

Ferreting out the sanity
Twixt incoherent brambles,
I responded only
To the goodness therein.

"I see you've had
A really rough time.
I'm sure I caused
A lot of that pain.

Could you meet me
In that restaurant
Near Fisherman's Wharf?
Perhaps we can set it straight."

She promptly answered,
"Seven pm Saturday.
Would like to try
To mend it."

Saturday quickly came.
We talked late into the night.
It looks good to me.
I think we can square it around.

Oblique—not straightforward or direct (Macmillan Dictionary for Students)
*Opaque—So obscure as to be unintelligible. (American Heritage Dictionary)

Woman

She needs time by herself
To do her alchemy.*

She needs quiet time
With her spinning wheel
To spin straw
Into God knows what.

Give her the freedom
To nurture what she wishes.
Listen closely
To what she has to say.
You may be astounded.

Give her occasion
To weave the fabric
Of wifehood,
of motherhood,
womanhood,
and sisterhood.

Disturb her not.
Hurry her not.
Grant her the sacred
Time and space
To conjure,
to mend,
to engender,
knead,
mould,
and to heal.

Afford her time
At her special desk

With stationary
And pens.
Time with her music
Choreographing* destiny.

Time in her kitchen
Mustering* culinary* muses.*
Time with the children
Even when they are grown.
Time to create husband
Into his finest self.

Take great joy
As she wields her magic
And waves her wand
In the kitchen,
the bedroom,
the nursery,
the garden,
the studio,
the workplace,
the stage.

A woman is a world
Unto herself.
Afford her
Great respect.

Left to her
Own devices
She will create
Wonder without limit.

*Alchemy—Any seemingly magical power or process of transforming one thing into another
Macmillan Dictionary for Students
*Choreograph—to plan (an event or complex course of action) in careful detail
Webster's New World College Dictionary

Mustering—to gather or call (troops) together
Culinary—relating to cooking
Muses—spirit or other source of genius or artistic inspiration
Macmillan Dictionary for Students

Wife

I want to reacquaint you
With the wonder that is you,
The joy of having you to talk to.
Constant desire to see us through.

The kindnesses rendered unseen.
The hours spent with the children,
Caring for Grandpa in between.
Appreciate more than you'd imagine.

Reading stories aloud at bedtime.
In the kitchen teaching her to cook.
Gathering wildflowers in springtime.
Helping him on how to bait a fishhook.

All these little things day by day,
Listening, teaching and learning too.
Magnitude of gratitude wish to convey.
This acknowledgement is long overdue.

Listen to Your Wife

Listen to your wife!
There is something
She is trying
To get across
To you.

Listen to her closely!
She may not speak it
In so many words.
It's a perception
Of a gesture,
A specific
Kind of sigh,
Something about an aching,
Some kind of longing.
You don't miss
This kind of stuff.

Be alert!
Your wife is speaking
If only by the incline
Of her head
Or a tiny puffiness
Around her lips,
Semblance* of a pout.
Or an almost
Imperceptible
Dimming of the light
Emanating from her.

Don't miss these signs!
She is trying
To tell you something.

Even she may not
Be able to articulate it.
But it means the earth
For her to be understood.

Pay attention!
She's talking
To you.
Put your ear
To the ground
Beneath her feet.

Hear her!
This intensity
Of listening
Is the soul
Of love.
Take time for this.
Care about this a lot.
It matters!

*Semblance—the barest trace
American Heritage Dictionary

Love to Me

It is the passion of the first stirring and the intensity of admiration that remains with us as a steadfast continuance.

As it grows and matures it becomes an abiding support for each other, ruggedly there for the long run.

It is a constant tenderness that deepens with the years accompanied by a muscular loyalty and appreciation that just won't quit.

It is a shared mutual joy that stands firm through all seasons.

Love, the Later Years

It is being able to utterly astound
Each other after all these years
With an observation, a perception,
Or something unexpected said.

It is the enduring excitement
Of life shared despite
The corporeal* realities
Of aging human bodies.

It is the amazement
Mutually experienced.
The spiritual vision
Growing keener daily
Regardless of the failings
Of physical perceptions.

*Corporeal—of the body or of the nature of the body; not spiritual; mortal
Macmillan Dictionary for Students

Twenty-four Years

Together now coming upon
Nine thousand days.
Admire you in
As many ways.
Appreciate the great
And little things
You constantly do.
Cherish the marriage.
Cherish you.

⌣⌐

Silver

For a quarter of a century
You have been a joy for me.
Wish to explain how I love you.
It's what you assist me to be.
You have an uncanny ability
To find beauty inside of me,
Beauty even I can't see.
For this, I deeply respect you.
You have helped me limitlessly.
Twenty five years of high level fun,
More fun than's legal under any sun.
You've backed me up in every way.
Because of this I am alive today.
A quarter century of constant care,
Keeping me sane, healthy and there.
I so appreciate your nurture.

⌣⌐

Coming on Thirty Years

I give thanks for the vast tenderness
With which our marriage is blessed.
I appreciate the constancy.
Joyous days you've spent with me.
The shared fun of creating a life.
I am very proud to call you my wife.

⌣⟶

Turning Sixty-five

*(Dedicated to my wife, Connie,
on the occasion of her 65th Birthday 13 May 2012)*

It's my honor
To have helped you survive
This life's challenges
To staying sane and alive.
You're inspiration.
You are loveliness.
You're Imagination.
The wondrous muse
Of my creation.

Thank you for these years
Of listening to me
With a thousand ears,
Helping me to see
Purpose of my life,
My own destiny.
For each of these things
Thank you infinitely.
You have helped me

Achieve the beauty in me,
To be the best I can be.
In this way shaped our destiny
And created our eternity.

Love for the Long Run

For Constance on Valentine's Day 2015

Above all it is the profound density
Of love experienced and expressed.
It is the unlimited richness and intensity
Of each living moment so blessed.

A willingness to constantly care.
Desire to be fully and utterly counted on.
The constant decision to stand in and be there.
To always be awake and aware; to forbear.

Continuing to listen, a willingness to hear,
An unrelenting complete attention.
An abiding ability to respect and revere.
Fully living each day together one by one.

The daily challenges to overcome.
Romance for the long run.
This is what an actual life can become.
This is life's victory hard won.

Love

To George and Diane about to marry at seventy

I wish to spend some delicious time with you
Lavishing profoundly felt communication on each other,
Listening to you with a fervent* intensity of hearing.

I intend to make you ridiculously happy,
To create a life with you of nearly inconceivable joy.
We will paint our days with flamboyant* colors,
Engendering inconceivable tenderness and softness in each other.

Gentle affirmation that we do live, that we possess beauty,
That we are of value and we do immeasurably matter.
This brings to the surface for each other the artistry
We are each individually capable of creating.

I relish the rich fabric of life we bestow on each other
As we live one more unrestrained day together.

Louis A. Swartz

With you I experience an unimaginable duplication of dreams.
We satiate* our uncontainable shared hunger for just plain fun.
We exchange mind-bursting ideas so that sparks fly from our faces.

We navigate each other through the loss, pain
And sometimes even horror of existence here on earth,
Doing the countless things that make life livable or even possible.
All the while recognizing the wonder in each other.

We do not miss the quietest concern scarcely voiced.
We draw out the greatness in each other in all conceivable ways
So that we become the finest ourselves we can be.

*Fervent—having or showing great warmth of feeling; intensely devoted or earnest
*Flamboyant—flame like or brilliant in form or color
*Satiate—to satisfy to the full; gratify completely
Webster's New World College Dictionary

Children

How in the world am I
To comprehend this child?
She sees the morning skies,
And the little things of life
Through extraordinary eyes.

Do you remember
Being a tiny boy
Yet filling the sky?

Louis A. Swartz

Newly Born

Once again to feel my baby softness
Against my mother's warmth
And to experience again
Mother's initial love.
Another beginning.
Another sojourn here.

Begin You Anew

We, who are forever being born,
We are the eternal beginners.
We didn't come to this place yester morn.
We're the continual voyageurs.
Oh earth! Oh life! Begin you anew.
So much to now learn, so much to do.

New growth: buds, shoots, sprouts constantly spring.
New skin of infant here one more time,
Child's new eyes newly opening,
It's bedtime with a nursery rhyme.
Oh earth! Oh life! Begin you anew.
So much to now learn, so much to do.

Wonderment

You need to retain your wonderment.
Time with the children is time well spent.

Brother Comes Home

Let me relay to you
The terrific
Experience
Of being alive.

The perception
Of a child
Newly born,
Intensity
Of awareness,
Strength
Of softness,
Freshness
Of new life.

Child's palpable* wonder,
"Where have I come?"
The world again
Through different eyes.

Morning sunlight
Through window,
Family dog respectfully
Watching, protecting
Near the door.
Father's
Uncontainable pride.
Mother's
Unbounded joy.

Grandma in noble
Attendance bedside
And in the kitchen,
Cooking, cleaning, fixing.

Warm heart bursting.
Grandpa delighted
And somewhat adrift.

In the distance
Sound of violin practice.
Children playing
Early morning soccer.

Kitchen smells,
Eggs cooking,
Coffee brewing,
Fresh bread baking.

Brother touches
Newborn's arm
Lightly with tenderness.
Instilled with awe.
Baby's eyes open.
Brother's face above.

The soccer children
Are silent.
Violin lesson ends.
All's quiet
In the nursery
And in the house.
New child sleeps.
Grace surrounds him.

Palpable—Capable of being touched or felt; tangible.
Macmillan Dictionary for Students

Child's Time

As a young child riding
On the circus merry-go-round,
I was able to wonder,
I was able to astound.

Memories of child's time,
Hearing the carnival sound.
In the bright days of childhood
The world was my playground.

When We Played with Wooden Toys

From a long and happy time ago
I remember our childhood's joys.
Sitting beneath the bay window
When we played with wooden toys.

It was a time filled full with family,
We were amazed, tiny girls and boys.
A time of infinite possibility,
When we played with wooden toys.

There was a grape arbor in Grandma's backyard.
Back porch strewn with toy horses and cowboys.
Pictures of wild horses painted on birthday card.
When we played together with wooden toys.

These were times of unending fun.
We'd giggle and make lots of noise.
Laughing outside in the summer sun.
When we played with wooden toys.

I would like to go there again
And find those girls and boys.
Reconstruct my wooden train
And play again with wooden toys.

The Tiny Boy

High topped leather
Child's shoes,
Broken toy soldier
Beneath the window,
Leaning on the wall.
Childhood's bed
Neatly made,
Pirate bedspread.

Oak near window,
Could nearly
Climb out on it.
I dreamed that I was
Bigger than the house,
That I was peeking
Into my window
From the outside.

Do you remember
Being a tiny boy
Yet filling the sky?

I saw the shoreline
And the ship lights
Out in the ocean.
Returning home
There were houses

On the hill
With tiny lights
Visible in the night.

"Mommy let me
Tell you where I went!"

"Get dressed now.
You'll be late for school."

I put on my shoes
One by one
On the edge of my bed
In my tiny room.

The light through the window,
The huge oak outside,
The broken toy soldier
Were all filled with life.

I felt so happy
Walking to school
A tiny bit
Above the ground
Remembering
The vast ocean
And the ship lights
In the night.

Louis A. Swartz

It's Big We Grow

I know what I know.
As lessons we learn,
It is big we grow.
It's how we return.

I'm a child now,
But not for long.
Yet I know how
To get along.

The things I can see,
The places I've known
Mean a lot to me.
Day by day I've grown.

I've a job to do
As soon as I'm large.
I'm here to help you.
One day I'll take charge.

Awe

A warm fall afternoon,
House in the country,
North of Boston,
On the porch reading.
My four year old son
Standing silently still
Beyond the Great Oak,
Near the grape arbor.
A doe, fawn at her side,
Standing before him,
Devoid* of movement,
Rapt* in mutual awe.

*Devoid—completely lacking
*Rapt—deeply moved or delighted
American Heritage Dictionary

Louis A. Swartz

Between 43rd Street and Eternity

Dedicated to my son.

They captured me
Somewhere between
43rd Street 'n eternity.

My childhood years were bitchin',
Living dangerously
On the run in Hell's Kitchen.

Raised on the streets of New York City.
The nuns kept me in line.
Taught me about the Holy Trinity.

While up on 48th the parents
Helped people go free.
This was the world for me,
Hell's Kitchen, New York City.

The streets were wild
Far beyond belief.
Didn't tell the parents much.
I didn't want to give them grief.

I was street wise
And fancy free.
First glimpse of the real world
New York City gave to me.

Hell's Kitchen, Manhattan,
Between 43rd street and eternity
Was childhood's home to me.

Years with which I was blessed.
Someday we'll have a beer
And I'll tell you the rest.

Holy

Leaning down to listen
To what the child has to say.
Seeing a son through illness.
A word of kindness
Ameliorating a loss.
A note of endearment
Left behind to lighten
A rough and harried day,
Message of encouragement.
Love when most needed.
These holy things.

Carnegie Park

Having walked here,
I remember there is
A turn in the road here
Where grow a profusion*
Of purple and pink lilacs.

This is where the old men
Have sat through the years,
Jawing to each other
About deeply felt losses
And personal triumphs
Not ever to be forgotten.

A little bit further up the road
An ancient trail has always led
To a meadow rimmed with oaks
Where children laugh and play
And roll in the soft meadow grass.

Louis A. Swartz

Here was a carousel long ago
With hand painted gallant horses
Of purple, pink, robin's egg blue.
Ice cream stand and ice cream man
Who scooped me a chocolate cone.

Late in the afternoon the old men sat
In woolen overcoats in the summer sun
With the lilac trees surrounding them,
Playing checkers and chess on stone tables.

I was a child here. I thought I would be
A child here forever in this lovely park.
These summers and these warm days,
It was as close to heaven as I've been.

*Profusion—Rich abundance
Noah Webster's 1828 Dictionary

The Children

Children who came here
With a special destiny
To create human harmony,
 A place men can walk free.

The time has now come
To put an end to strife.
Each person under the sun
Has a sacred right to life.

These are singular children
With an enormous job to do.
It is very hard to imagine
How much we depend on you.

Bless this noble crew
And the spirit they imbue.*
They know what to do.
A new world will ensue.*

*Imbue—inspire as with emotions, ideals
*Ensue—to occur as a consequence; result
Macmillan Dictionary for Students

Who Will Show It to a Child Just As It Is

Who will show it to a child
Exactly as it actually is?
Who will express without apology
It was permitted to come to this?

Shame of this evil bequeathment.*
Would that we would have been

Louis A. Swartz

A lot less permissive and tolerant
When our unlovely, profane* destiny
Was originally formed and styled.
We should have killed him dead
When the monster was a child.

It isn't time to analyze
Why we didn't perceive
The horror in his eyes
Or the intention behind
His well-crafted lies.

Never imagined
It would come to this.
Misestimated the venom
In the devil's kiss.

I know it does matter
That we tried and tried.
I just wish we'd been stronger
And that the monster had died.

As I pass this torch to you,
I can trust you, my child,
To see us fully through.
Oh, my God, please know
How much we count on you.

*Bequeathment—to pass (something) on to another; hand down
American Heritage Dictionary
*Profane—irreverent to anything sacred
Noah Webster's 1828 Dictionary

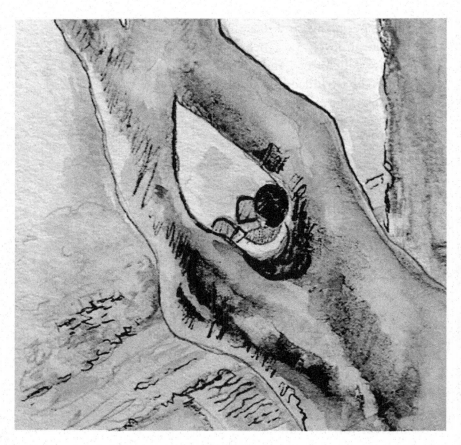

Bough

Halfway up the hillside was an
Enormous tree. It's massive
Roots entrenched deep inside
The precipitous* cliff upon
Which it made its home. Fifty
Meters round and ringed by
Broad boughs that jutted
A hundred feet out and
Were wide enough to walk on,
High above the valley below.

Louis A. Swartz

On one of these boughs there
Was a naturally hollowed
Out place, almost like a cave
Of wood, large enough for me
To crawl into and to be
Invisible.

It was here I would go to dream,
And remember.
It was here I would go
To leave the war,
The ugliness of the streets,
The stench of death,
The horror in the faces
Of the women, the disfigured
Faces of young girls.

I would go to the tree to
Dream and remember
Somehow another time before I
Was born. Not here. Not
Even near here. I could
So vividly remember this
Place.

A tiny village with lush
Fields surrounding.
Three old men – the farmer,
The holy man and the teacher
Sitting on their haunches
Drinking chai, telling
Stories of times that
Were gentler still, wondrous
Stories of sanctity* and
Healing.

Story of a mother
And a child and an
Agonizing birth and how
Magic and tenacity,*
Perseverance* and miracle
Somehow intervened
And brought mother and
Child back from the edge
Of demise.*

Lying in my wooden cave high
Above the forest floor,
I would remember. I drank
Deeply from this world
That once was,
A place pervaded by a
Seemingly unlimited
Decency.

The child was
Respected as the soul of
The future. The girls
And women, mothers and
Grandmothers were respected
As they carried the wisdom
Of the home and held
Together that world with
Their mother's love.

There was also great
Admiration of the men
Who planted the fields
And crafted and repaired
The implements of survival.

And finally, the elders
Above all, who passed on the

Balance and wonder,
Consideration* and humility,
Courage, reverence
And aesthetic that had
Been graciously passed
Down to them.

On my bough I would
Remember and dream.
If such a world once was,
It could be once again.
I was sure this was true.
But where do I begin?

I remembered the words
Of the old man, the teacher
And what he told
Us children.
"Each increment of kindness
Matters no matter how small.
In fact, these kindnesses
Matter more than anything
In the world."

Lying there in my tree
I thought about a young
Girl who unjustly had
Acid thrown in her face
By her parents. She had
Kissed a boy beneath the
Willow by the river.
This was her crime.
She would hide her scarred
Face and tried as hard as she
Could to lose herself from life.

I went and found her.
I told her I could see her
Soul and she was beautiful.
I told her it was okay she
Kissed the boy. She cried
A lot and then she smiled.
Even with the scars around
Her mouth, I had never seen
Anything as lovely as
That smile.

From then on I resolved to
Live like this. My purpose
Became to inspire
Helpfulness and sensitivity,
Openheartedness and gentleness
Into each moment of my
Life, just as we did then
In a time I remembered.

Precipitous—very steep; as a precipitous cliff or mountain
Noah Webster's 1828 Dictionary
Sanctity—goodness; purity; godliness
Tenacity—extreme persistence in adhering to or doing something; relentlessness
American Heritage Dictionary
Perseverance—continuing in some effort, course of action, etc. in spite of difficulty, opposition...
Demise—ceasing to exist; death
Webster's New World College Dictionary
Consideration—thoughtful or appreciative regard for others; respect
Macmillan Dictionary for Students
Increment—the process of increasing in number, size, quantity or extent
American Heritage Dictionary

Street Scene

Walking with my son on New York street,
His passion to know was evident.
Together with him I felt complete.
The utter joy of our own time spent
Sharing mutual astonishment.

Guy playing the sax on Forty-Third.
Old man sitting in the news stand.
Unfamiliar languages overheard.
Walking with my young son hand in hand,
Could feel him trying to understand.

He studied the people passing by
With more interest than I'd ever seen.
He'd speak right to them. He wasn't shy.
The businessman, housewife and drag queen,
He eagerly took in the street scene.

Saw a man asleep in a doorway.
My son stopped dead and looked at the man.
He looked up. I didn't know what to say.
"He has no place to live..." He began,
"...We've got to help him any way we can."

A Child's Right

These children are an exceptional lot.
They've learned from birth to be superlative.*
Self-respect and dignity can be taught.
Help, compassion, and kindness are native.
School them in discernment* to cause insight.
Real education is a child's right.

*Superlative—of the highest order, quality or degree
*Discernment—keenness of perception, judgment or understanding; insight
American Heritage Dictionary

WOW!

Claire* painted a bird filled with loveliness
From imagination when she was three
Of a world to which she'd gained ingress.*
Face flushed, glowing, she handed it to me.
Wonderstruck, captivated and wordless
The painting inspired vast joyousness.

Sought an appropriate acknowledgement
For the image that was laid before me,
A recognition of accomplishment,
Validation of her ability.
To say all this to a child somehow.
I settled on a gigantic WOW!

*Claire—There is a character or person who appears several times in this volume and once in Volume One of Constructed of Magic. To dispel any mystery, I wanted to say who this is. Claire is someone from my imagination. She represents kindness, aesthetics and passion for life. She is written as a child, an artist, a wife, a mother and a grandmother. She has an enormous appreciation of life. I am happy to introduce her to you.
*Ingress— Power of entering; means of entrance
Noah Webster's 1828 Dictionary

Louis A. Swartz

My Child's Eyes

How in the world am I
To comprehend this child?
She sees the morning skies,
And the little things of life
Through extraordinary eyes.

She's learned from ancient teachers
Marvels that once were known.
She's able to understand the creatures.
She told me she has another home
Somewhere recalled by her alone.

Last night she brought me a stone to see.
Told me it contained great beauty.
Said there were a thousand colors therein.
I strained to see, but it was gray to me.
She said, "Mommy, you just need to imagine."

Day by lovely day raising this child,
Learning so much more than I teach,
Being shown worlds vast and wild.
Amazed, astonished, willingly beguiled,*
Begin to see through the eyes of my child.

*Beguile—to amuse or charm; delight or fascinate
American Heritage Dictionary

{ 3 }

Grandmothers, Grandfathers, Mothers and Fathers

I can make anything in my kitchen.
Heaven meets earth somewhere
between my dry goods pantry and
my treasured glass baking dishes.

Grandmother of forever, may
your love pervade the future
now and always.

Daddy

Early morning on a Saturday,
I was down in the basement with Dad.
We were building a village made of clay.
The great joy in his face made me glad.
It was the very best time I'd ever had.

He made houses, horses, cars and trees,
All the while laughing hard with me.
He sculpted clay with incredible ease.
His utter happiness was plain to see.
This way I always want him to be.

I think I was a bit shy of five.
Was early spring, beginning of May.
I have never seen Daddy so alive.
I'll always, ever remember that day,
When Dad came to the basement to play.

Grandpa

To my Grandpa Green

Grandpa sitting on the sofa
in the living room,
stiff and alone.
When he worked
at Bridgeville Trust
for fifty years,
he would wake
at 5:30 am to arrive
at the Bank on time.
Now, living with family,
retired from the Bank,
he still wakened
at 5:30 am,
Dressed in his blue,
three piece suit
complete with his
gold retirement
pocket watch.
He would come
downstairs
to the sofa
and sit there
all day long.

The men from the Old Country
With whom he spoke in Hungarian,
French, Italian, Spanish, German
And perhaps a little Yiddish,
No longer came to him
To do their banking.
Grandma was long since gone.
He knew he'd not be here long.

Louis A. Swartz

He could feel death in his legs.
He was proud of his years at the bank.
    And of his three daughters.
He missed his old blue '57 Chevy.
    And the grape arbor out back.
He missed the fresh apple pie,
Hot from the oven Grandma made.

He had not planned on growing old.
He had not prepared for death.
"You live on in the acts of goodness
You performed," the Rabbi had said.
He remembered something vague
About "The Kingdom of Heaven."
None of it made much sense to him.

He knew he was soon to die.
He did not have knowledge
Of what would become of him.
He had a numb, apathetic terror
Personal to him of which
He could not speak to anyone.

In the afternoon his Grandson
Returned home from school.
He went straight to his Grandpa.
He wanted to show him an elephant
He had painted at school.
The best elephant Grandpa ever saw.

The boy sat up close to Grandpa
And said, "I was once old like you."
Grandpa was startled by the earnestness
Of the child's communication.
The boy continued with great intensity,
"Then I died, but everything was ok."

The child ran off to play with his brother
Leaving Grandpa with his thoughts.
He was trying to get his wits around
What the child had just told him.
Somehow he felt extremely calm,
Thinking of what the child had said.

The numb terror eased away.
Perhaps there was something
To the words of the child.
An awareness awakened,
The possibility of a future.
Finally, he let out a deep belly laugh.

My Kitchen

I can make anything in my kitchen.
Heaven meets earth somewhere
between my dry goods pantry
and my treasured glass baking dishes.

Wooden countertop where
I chop the greens,
Dice the onions,
Weave the dreams.

A singular magic
Woven into my casserole.
It feeds the body
And touches the soul.

Come into my kitchen
From the bitter cold.
It is in my kitchen
Wondrous stories are told.

Louis A. Swartz

Have a mug of hot cider
Spiked with cinnamon.
The child's eyes grow wider
As you, your stories spin.

My kitchen transforms
Folks into what they ain't.
The meanest old man
Can turn into a saint.

It was in my kitchen
My sister fell in love
With a lovely, giant man,
His hand big as a boxing glove.

Heaven meets earth
As I toss the salad
And dinner's given birth.

When Saul Died

For Saul Epstein

Take not away
An old man's dreams.
Listen to him closely
As he sits toothless
And amazed
Before you
On a summer morning
In Brooklyn
Before dawn.

"I was chosen
From seven thousand
School children.
My God!
Could I sing.
See this medal,
Ribbon's frayed,
So pretty, yes?"

"There are still
People who
Remember
The sweetness
Of my voice.

When Saul died
The Cantor asked me
To sing the Kaddish.*
Wasn't a dry eye
In the house.

If you can stay
A few more minutes
There's a thing
I'd like to tell you...

OK...perhaps
Another time...
I know the traffic
Can be heavy
On The Williamsburg.*
You should get going."

*Kaddish—Jewish prayer for the dead
*Williamsburg Bridge—A New York City bridge connecting the Boroughs
of Manhattan and Brooklyn

Louis A. Swartz

Cookbook

It was the spring of 1950,
when I was twenty, when my
Grandmother gave me her
cook book. She had just turned
ninety three. She told me she
had started it when she was
a girl like me, nearly twenty.
"Wait 'til I'm gone a while
before you open it and have a
look." I did exactly as
she said.

Alone in early morning light
I opened the book with trembling
hands. Woven into the pages
were colors picked up by
the sunlight. Magic and
memories between the recipes,
home truths of eternal sanity.

Love note to grandpa between
the recipe for her marvelous grape
leaf casserole and the one
for hot apple cider made
from green Granny Smith apples.
Unrestrained expression
of how she loved him so.

Autumn leaves pressed
between the pages. There
were home spun poems she
had written for the kitchen
(and the ages).

Grainy photos of children
playing with wooden toys.
Children long since grown
and passed. Yellowed
recipes for pies and stews
and roasts and stuffings
and soups.

More love letters suffused*
with innocence and surprising
passion. Verse clipped from
newspapers 60 years ago,
seed packets for garden
vegetables and flowers,
clipped newspaper articles
of pathos* and heroism.

Letters of a child who
went to The War in Europe
in 1915 and did not return
neatly folded into the
folio pockets of her cookbook.

Birth and marriage announcements,
obituaries, an ad for
a hat sale 47 years ago.
There were ads for fine
face soap and girdles, slips
and sweaters, cleansers
and miraculous detergents.

Dried flowers pressed
between the pages, messages
to herself written 55 years ago.
Notes of condolence, shopping
lists, report cards, drawings

by her children, prayers,
reminders.

There were letters
from Auntie Grace in England,
a letter from a first grade
teacher concerned with
behavior.

There was an ad for
Grandpa's confectionary
store. Beneath that graduation
pictures, prom pictures with
tuxes and gowns, corsages
and boutonnieres.

Christmas cards with gold
and silver sprinkles, movie
show ticket stubs.

There were faded pictures
of the old family house,
the garden, the fence, the
oak tree.

She had handwritten
home remedies for colds, flu,
sunburn and aches and
bruises.
More notes written to herself
about her losses – a child
who was never born, grandpa's
misadventures, her dreams of
a place in the country, to be
a dancer, her joys – birth
of daughter and son

and the myriad things she
found funny and sad and
cherishable. There was even
a song she wrote about "The
Great War" and never finished.

The book, made of old
leather, stuffed to eight
inches thick, marvelous
to touch, soft and warm.
It was as if Grandma
had left her soul behind
which over the years now
has become a part of
mine.

Suffuse—to spread through or over, as with a light, color or emotion
Pathos—quality, as in an event or work of art, that arouses a feeling of pity, sadness or compassion
Macmillan Dictionary for Students

Mothers

You walked here
And carried water.
In the valley below
You gave birth
And nursed your child.
This matters.

With the strength
Of your hands you
Worked these fields.
You fed the children
And kept a clean house.

You walked upright
And taught the children
To walk upright.
This matters.

You sewed the clothes.
You cared for your man,
Loved him and watched
Over him as he slept.
This matters.

In the moments left
You cared for Grandma.
Pouring water for her
When her throat was parched
And there was no water
To be found.
This matters.

On the river rocks
You washed the clothes
And dried them
In the sun.
You imparted
To the children
They were loved
And had value
And that you were
So happy they were here.
This matters.

You came here,
Dreamed here,
Loved here,
Worked here
And taught here.
This matters.

All of this,
Every hour of it,
Every day of it,
No matter how rough sometimes,
No matter how apparently
Thankless it has been,
Matters.

No matter your hands
Are raw and calloused,
That your legs are bowed,
That your breasts sag
From childbearing
And heavy labor over decades.

That you have attended the births,
That you have swept the ashes
From the funeral biers,
That you prayed here,
All of this, each and every
Act of nurturance
And devotion,
Each labor
And sacrifice,
Each pain endured,
Matters.
Matters enormously.
Matters incalculably.

These things you have done here
For people for whom you have cared,
The children you have
Taken to your breast,
These things actually,
When the prayers

Have been said,
When the ashes
Have been swept,
When the tears
Have been cried,
When the eyes
Have been dried,
When all has been
Said and done,
These labors and cares
And loves that you purveyed
Are all that matters
At all.

Elephants Never Die

Elephant, lovely creature,
Legend said he could fly,
That he was immortal.
Elephants never die.
They become weightless
And ascend to the sky.

Least that was the tale
That Grandma told.
Stuck to her story
'Til she was very old.

Sometimes, noble and grand
Outside Grandma's window
Elephant would silently stand.
Was always just before dawn.

Grandma could clearly understand
Why the giant creature had come
On that particular morning
Just before the rising sun.
Grandma didn't explain it
To me or to anyone.

As she stood and spoke to him
I swear I could clearly see
The great elephant grin
And I'm sure he winked at me.

Then he turned around
Without a sound
And headed for home
In the elephant ground.

Tears of unrestrained joy
In my Grandma's eyes,
Something enormous
Just realized.

My Grandma smiled,
"The future is good!
Come with me child,
Let's gather some wood."

The elephants are walking.
The elephants are talking.
Nothing is as it seems.
The elephants are dreaming
Enormous elephant dreams.

My Dad

Four years old with Mother in the car,
Picking up Daddy from the bar.
3 AM said the clock on the sign.
Daddy was sad and smelled of wine.
We drove home along the streetcar line.

They thought I was long since asleep.
Was the first time I'd seen my Dad weep.
"Hate the bar! Want to live another way
 And make things of paint, plaster and clay,
But that seems impossible and faraway."

"There's something inside of me that's dead."
Jones and Laughlin Steel Mill glowing red.
Passed a big, red trolley on the right.
Saw sleepy folks in the streetcar light.
"I'm unable to resolve this tonight."

"I'm in a spiritual free-fall,
Spending my time selling alcohol.
I know I'm very far from a saint.
I have hardly practiced self restraint.
Permit me just this—the chance to paint!"

Months later I went to the cellar.
There were paint brushes in a Mason Jar.
A many colored light filled the space.
Absolute happiness in his face,
Dad was painting in a state of grace.

Grandma

To my Grandma, "Mammy"

Grandma,
If I
Could see it
Just for
A moment
Through your eyes,

So kindly
After all
These years,
Immortal
Patience,
Tolerance
Of the soul.

Grandma
Watching
From her
Living room
Chair.
Her blanket
On her lap,
Warmth in
Her eyes.

Knotted fingers
Still in her lap.
Exuding a grace
Unremembered
Here in this place.

Immortal while here
And yet still
Willing to
Wash the dishes.

Grandmother Eternal

Your patient hands
Folded in your lap.
I remember these,
But not as hands,
Semblance of a soul,
Eternal imprint.
It was the same majesty,
And kindness that filled
Your lovely, weathered face.

Your gentle hands
Immortally folded.
Expression in your eyes
Transcending lives,
Transcending cultures,
Transcending nations.

A brief glance
Into your ancient face,
Ten thousand years
In your bright, bright eyes.

You walked the earth
As one woman,
As all women,
Human and sacred history.

You are carrying water
Across the deserts
Of African continent.

You are washing clothes
In the river in India.
You wear pastel saris

Of pinky blue lavender,
Light purple, purple pink.
You gather manure for cooking fire.

You are Africa's mother
Giving birth in a village hut.

You are a thousand mourners
Walking in utter silence
Behind countless coffins
Of senseless death.
You are grandma ever watching
There as well.
Ten thousand years of future
In your kind and saddened eyes.

Grandmother Eternal
Bless this future
As you have blessed the past.

May your ancient eyes
Witness finally
Change of magnitude,
Vast change for good.
Grandmother of forever
May your love pervade
The future now and always.

Grandma, Sit with Me Awhile

Grandma, How I adore you.
Human warmth woven
into the folds of
the blanket around you
to keep you from the cold.
Graceful angel, I so
admire your forbearance.
Angel walking amongst us
in gossamer* flesh, barely
grounded here any more
at all. Sprinkles of wisdom
sparkling in your eyes and
around the corners of your
mouth. Ironies of the ages
in your subtle smile. Grandma,
sit here with me a while.
Grandma, barely human,
loosely tethered to the
earth. Ethereal* body scarcely
with us, nearly cast off.
Precious moment, while you
are still here and well
beyond in the same instant.

Grandma, sit with me by
the window as the evening
wells up beyond the
curtains. Stay with me
here awhile. I have
mighty need of your
pervasive comfort.
Sit with me here a while.

Louis A. Swartz

Gossamer—Light, thin, and filmy
Webster's New World College Dictionary
Ethereal—Extremely light or delicate: of the celestial spheres; heavenly: spiritual or otherworldly
American Heritage Dictionary

Newborn Wakens

Below the window newborn sleeping.
Outside sun rising above orchard,
White apple blossoms of early spring.
Her brothers playing in the backyard.

Mother readies herself for feeding.
The nursery's in perfect order.
Mother is above cradle smiling,
Patiently waiting for her to stir.

Nursery now filled with warm sunlight.
Baby's eyes open in amazement.
Sees mama's face and knows she's all right.
Their silence is soft and eloquent.

He Never Began to Live

It was with a halting hand
Daddy essayed* to draw a man.
What a joy he had from art,
But he was unable to begin.
It wasn't about the alcohol.
When he lost his personal pride
Was when he ceased to live.
There was beauty in his hands.
He wished to create loveliness.
He was just distracted by life.
Was not a tragedy he died.
It was he never began to live.

*Essayed—effort or attempt to do something; endeavor
Macmillan Dictionary for Students

Louis A. Swartz

Meeting

I will be there on the twenty forth
As you wrote in your lovely note.
What a joy to return to the North.
See you at the dock near the ferryboat,
The old steel pier where we used to fish.
To see you has been my fondest wish.

You will have grown very big I know
And won't be the child I recall.
But old men do age and children grow.
I heard you were over six feet tall.
I cannot describe in any degree
What this time with you will mean to me.

{ 81 }

{ 4 }

Human Sanctity

You cannot order compassion, benevolence,
forbearance, charity, kindness, tolerance, grace,
warm heartedness, humanity, humaneness, reason,
inclusion. For these things are the things of the heart,
the things of the spirit. The laws of man cannot
legislate the spirit.

Benevolence, Kindness.
Human Harmony, America, Humane Heritage

These Dreams Are

These dreams are the affirmation*
Of human possibility.
They are the illumination*
Of a purpose formed anciently.

These dreams are the realization,
The strived for restoration
And ultimate reclamation*
Of our beleaguered* Nation.

These dreams are the recognition
Of the innate divinity
That forms the human foundation
Vital to our ascendancy.*

These dreams are the long intended
Cessation of enduring loss,
The prayers we ardently left
In the crevices of the cross.

*Affirmation—Something declared to be true
American Heritage Dictionary
*Illumination—an enlightening of the understanding by knowledge, or the mind by spiritual light
Noah Webster's 1828 Dictionary
*Reclamation—a reclaiming or being reclaimed. Reclaim—to rescue or bring back (a person or people) from
error, vice, etc to ways of living or thinking regarded as right;
Webster's New World College Dictionary
*Beleaguered—to harass; beset (to attack from all sides)
American Heritage Dictionary
*Ascendancy—(The act of ascending or having ascended) Ascend—to go or move upward; rise; to rise from
a lower level or station; advance
American Heritage Dictionary

Perhaps

Perhaps there are
Benevolent creatures
Who live among us
Unsure to which world
They actually belong.

They move between
The temporary
And the eternal
With equal aplomb*
Maintaining friendships
In all worlds,
Assisting us
In all ways possible.

Aplomb—Complete self-confident assurance: poise
American Heritage Dictionary

White Sails in the Western Wind

We are no longer alone
While we stand by the sea
On tiptoes on sand and stone
Squinting in the sun to see
A tall ship to take us home.

End to human agony?
Can this actually be?
Waken sleeping humanity.
We can change our destiny
To a sane eternity.

Louis A. Swartz

You can bring all the people
To the far edge of the sea.
We know it is possible
To have human harmony
And restore our dignity.

White sails in the Western Wind.
We are free to hope again.
We can cast off our sorrow.
A new world can begin,
Our created tomorrow.

Long endured adversity*
Can now become supplanted
By abiding amity.*
Time of possibility,
A fulfillment finally
Of the strong urge to be free.

White sails in the western wind,
We are no longer alone.
We can start to breathe again.
We're ecstatic to the bone.
Tall ship comes to take us home.

*Adversity—condition or instance of misfortune, hardship or suffering
Macmillan Dictionary for Students
Amity—peaceful relations, as between nations; friendship
American heritage Dictionary

What Is Required of Me?

There is something I am unable
To fully understand and actually see.
What good, here on earth, can I enable?
When all has passed what is my destiny?
In this lifetime and for all eternity,
What, in truth, is required of me?

At the far edge of the meadow
Was a noble stand of oak trees.
There is something that they know.
Standing staunch, strong, at peace,
They seem aware of why they're there.
Perhaps there's truth they can bring to bear.

But what of me and my job here?
I stand beneath the oaks in cool shade
Willing a personal purpose to appear.
I'm responsible for mistakes I've made.
While I am here for this very short span,
I want only to do the level best I can.

Perhaps it is to stand firm like the oak tree,
To help my fellows every way I can.
Maybe this is something expected of me.
To care for my brothers to the very last man.
To give good counsel and listen attentively,
To help the people live with truth and clarity.

To stand strong and to continue to be there
When things are gentle and things are rough,
To keep on listening and to continue to care.
To help more when I think I've helped enough.
To do all I can to end human want and cruelty.
I think that's a start of what is required of me.

Louis A. Swartz

On The Side of the Angels*

Above all it is remaining constant
'Spite the convulsions of daily living.
On a deadened earth staying sentient.*
Able to persist through almost anything.
Weathering the trials of an earthling.

There is no way to dilute my love of man.
Know, at times, he can be petty and mean.
However, each individual lifespan
Contains heart and goodness often unseen.
What matters most is the help he has been.

It's imperative I remain steadfast
No matter how frightening it becomes.
Kindness begins to emerge at long last.
Man decides if he survives or succumbs.
I'm on the angel's side whatever comes.

* On the side of the angels — Supporting the good side. (This expression was coined by Benjamin Disraeli in 1864 in a speech about Darwin's theory that man is descended from the apes:"The question is this: Is man an ape or an angel? Now I am on the side of the angels." Before long it was extended to broader use, specifically to the moral view.)
American Heritage Dictionary of Idioms
*Sentient—having the faculty of perception
Noah Webster's 1828 Dictionary

This Sacred Ground

This sacred ground
Where we walk.
There were stone steps,
An open courtyard,
A venerable* oak
Beside a clear stream.

What occurred
In this place?

What magic
Was rendered?
Who came here
And what was learned?

There was a man,
Sainted and holy,
Who taught here
Long, long ago.
He taught lessons
Of the sanctity of man.

He taught that each
Person matters
Without exception.
Each and all have
The right of creation
And the right to love.

That a man does not die.
He continues
Life to life.
He has the privilege
Of determining
His personal future.

He taught us
Of a tenderness
For each other
We were capable
Of experiencing
Without limit.

We learned these lessons.
We will keep them
For a thousand years

And then longer.
These cherished wonders
Imparted to us.

We retain these truths
And hold them dear.
They are our heritage.
And our trust,
Our future
    And eternity.

Venerable—Venerable---deserving respect or reverence as by reason of age, character or position
Macmillan Dictionary for Students

Reminders

I had need of reminders—

That I am alive.
That I have a history,
Not just a past.
That there is future.
That it matters
I have come.

Reminders—

That beauty exists.
That there is kindness
In the world
And goodness
In the hearts of man.

Louis A. Swartz

Reminders—

That I came here
For a reason.
That there is sacredness
In communication.
There is nobility
Of the soul.

Reminders—

That my fellows
Do matter.
Their dreams,
      their happiness,
              their joys
matter.

Reminders—

That we will make it.
All will come out okay.
And we will all
Be glad we've come
And victory
Will be achieved.

An Angel Does Not Need to Be Taught

The angel does not need to be taught
Kindness, mercy, grace,
Tenderness of heart.
These are native.

In springtime
The flowers know
To bloom profusely
On the hill sides
And in the valleys.
This is native.

The angel needs just
To be left alone
To do her work.

A man knows goodness.
He knows mercy,
Courtesy, decency,
Humility and mindfulness.
They are native.

A man just needs
To be left alone
To do his work.
His kind heart
Is inborn and forever.

His brotherly love
Is integral
To how he's made.
A sense of justice
Is inherent.

Left alone the acorn
Ultimately becomes
The giant oak.

The beauty of angels,
The aesthetic of man,
The grace of creatures,
The artistry of flowers—
All this is of basic nature
Given time and space
And caring nurture
All of this will
Manifest and prevail.
We are blessed
That this is so.

Nine Thousand Years of Peace

The voices that were silenced
Will speak yet once again:
The humane,
The healers, the helpers,
Those with vision
And empathy, tolerance,
Charity* and responsibility.

Those who you thought
Were lost will again
Walk amongst you.

They will speak again
Of trust and care,
Respect and helpfulness,
Altruism* and honor
For each person
Who lives on this earth.

This is the age of healing.
You are, each and all,
Welcome here,
Respected here,
Cherished here.

You have buried
Your desire for vengeance.
You have no score
To settle.
It is over.
Finally over.

May a vast time
Of healing commence.
May the wounds
Be knitted up.
May the camps
Be overgrown
With flowers
And brambles.

This is a time
Of universal
Inclusion.
Trust prevails
Person to person
Everywhere.
Nine thousand years
Of peace
Will now commence.

*Charity—that disposition of the heart which inclines men to think favorably of their fellow men and to do them good
Noah Webster's 1828 Dictionary
*Altruism—unselfish concern or devotion to the welfare of others
Macmillan Dictionary for Students

How it Feels in their Skin

The fleeing, the broken, hurt and lost,
Listen closely to the stories they tell
Of the unwelcome frontiers they crossed
While escaping obliteration,*
Searching for an accepting nation.

Some of their friends were killed as they slept.
Some of their neighbors were lost at sea.
They lie in rough fields, cold and windswept.
A walking human catastrophe
Unparalleled in recent memory.

Understand how it feels in their skin.
In the face of such atrocity
Apathy is always the worst sin.
Innate human generosity
Is a true, vital necessity.

*Obliteration—to remove or destroy completely so as to leave no trace
American Heritage Dictionary

America My Country #3

America, my country
I begin you again
As I could begin you
A thousand times.

Do I mourn you?
No! No way!
Somewhere you have
Lost your compass.*

At your inception
There was an openhearted
Belief in the sanctity
Of each living person.

No nation ever had
A more honest birth.
We made a promise
To the people of earth.

It had to do with liberty
And the personal nobility
Of all of our people
Regardless of station.

America, my country
I begin you again
As I could begin you
A thousand times.

Such a thirst for change,
A longing to regain
The original intentions
Upon which we were founded.

We have lost touch
With the founding dream.
We walk now
With a broken dignity.

We have forgotten
Our brotherly respect.
Somehow we've grown
Hard and callous.

Once, in the eyes
Of my son,

I saw infinite
Future and possibility.

Somewhere along the way
There was a betrayal
Of terrific magnitude.
We lost our bearings.

These streets are not
Familiar to me.
I do not recognize
These vacant faces.

There is a coldness here
I do not remember.
This is not the country
I once knew.

Who are these people,
Heads down and separate
Walking past me
With hollowed out hearts?

    America, my country
    I begin you again
    As I could begin you
    A thousand times.

Where is the warmth
Of my Nation?
The unconditional
Welcome I recall?

I sense a hunger
In the land
For the friendship
We once knew.

Gather now at the table,
Bow your heads
And give thanks
For our country.

The people of this world
Yearn for the human regard
That was basic to our
Original creation.

>America, my country
>I begin you again
>As I could begin you
>A thousand times.

The intention
Was the creation
Of a free
And equal nation.

This purpose
Still lives with us
And can still
Be achieved.

Remember! The care
And inclusion with which
We were founded.
It's all still there.

We are far from lost.
There's an American future.
It will take some major sweat
To get us back on the rails.

>America, my country
>I begin you again

As I could begin you
A thousand times.

Just remember
The goodness
That engendered
This fine nation.

The positive spirit
With which we were born
Cannot be destroyed
As long as we remember.

Mankind needs for us
To be our kind selves
And to be the America
Originally promised.

Compass—awareness or understanding of one's purpose or objectives
American Heritage Dictionary

Louis A. Swartz

America, my Country #4

America, my country
I begin you again.
There is an *esprit**
It is vital to regain.

Looking for a country
That is honest and sane.
In betrayal's false face,
The dreams dreamt still remain.

It is quite true that some
Have plenty to explain.
But whatever may come,
We've our honor to retain.

America, my country
I begin you again.
The rumbling harmony
Of the midnight train.

Sitting in a diner
In a Midwest town,
Some things we require
To turn upside down.

Hoping for an insight.
Coffee and conversation,
How do we set it right
And restore our nation?

America, my country
I begin you again.
It looks quite rough to me
To get back where we've been.

A trucker ordered hotcakes.
"Have to stay the night here
While they fix my brakes.
Can't believe what I hear."

Sat down in front of me
And took a giant bite.
I sipped my black coffee.
He whispered as if to the night,
"We can't go down without a fight."

America, my country
I begin you again.
Our purpose is to be free.
But in the quiet of the Midwest night
We can't go down without a fight.
Can't go down without a fight.

*Espirit—Liveliness of mind or spirit—Espirit de corps—feeling of mutual regard existing in a group and its members that are all working together toward some common goal.
Macmillan Dictionary for Students*

Lore

*Lore — Definition American Heritage Dictionary, Fifth edition: Accumu-
lated knowledge or beliefs held by a group about a subject especially when
passed from generation to generation by oral tradition.*
*Derivation: Indo European root leis — Track, furrow / Old English last,
sole, footprint / Old English laesten, to continue. From Germanic laistjan
"to follow a track" / Old English lar, learning / From Germanic liz non to
follow a course (of study) From Latin lira, furrow*

We walked this earth.
Our footprints remain.
We broke bread,
Experienced love
And gave birth.

We plowed furrows,
Planted the crops,
Built the temples,
Buried our dead.
Can this be lost?

Imprint in the sand,
A man with a burden.
There was blood let.
There's a trail to follow.
Message left behind
For the future to find.

A faint trail,
All that remains.
Each of us matters,
Our names may be forgotten
But we are not gone.

A soldier stood guard here.
Below musicians gathered.
Hallowed songs were sung.
Laughter echoed to the hills.
We celebrated the harvest.
Young people fell in love.

Here we taught the children.
Wisdom was passed on to them.
They learned human kinship
And the honor of their people.

Footprint moist with tears.
Bare imprint of child.
Ruts and furrows,
Images and echoes,
Bleached bones,
Ancient beads
And earthen urns,
Remembrance
Of our sojourn
In this place.

Stories passed down
Of heroes and gods,
Of holy men
And humble men,
Of mother's anguish
And triumph,
Of sons who returned
And those who
Stayed behind.
Impressions of magic
And worship.

Louis A. Swartz

We've shed our earthly shells
And left our terror behind
And our joy and glory as well.

We nursed our children
And tended them in sickness.
Over these graves we wept
And gave respect and homage.
We practiced humaneness
And day after day did our job.

There remains
Still a vestige,*
An impress,*
A foot print.
Each imprint matters.
Each was and is
A living soul.
And each of us will
Walk again.

*Vestige—trace, sign or perceptible evidence of something that once existed but no longer exists
*Impress—to form or make a mark
Macmillan Dictionary for Students

Drawing Out the Magnificence

Stirred by the immense
Joy of being alive,
The continual excitement,
The unrestrained amazement.
Looking for the magnificence
In each man walking,
Drawing out his specialness.
Doing this as a way of life,
As a reason for living.

Making each individual child, woman
And each man welcome here.
They are valuable.
They have something
To give, to contribute.
They have a place.
And all the while constantly
Nurturing their wonder,
Drawing out their beauty,
Drawing out their magnificence.

Rights Sacred and Divine

We are the children
Who walk this earth.
We matter.
We can create something beautiful.
We have a place.
It is alright that we are here.

We can be loved,
    respected,
        admired.

Afforded dignity,
        courtesy,
            kindness.

We may be a little different
In body, in language, in belief.
This is all right.
We can be given sanctuary.

Permit us safe passage
on every trail,
Every road,
           every highway.

Safe passage on the rivers
And the oceans.

And right down to the littlest,
Scrawny, odd and funny lookin' kid,
We can be loved,
     can be part of it,
           cared for,
                supported,
                     looked after,
                          bothered with.

We have importance,
           value,
                beauty,
                     worth,
                          substance,
                               position.

There's something in us
To be admired.
We have personal pride
And self-respect.
We are okay.

We can learn.
We can read the books,

Louis A. Swartz

Learn music and writing.
We can learn about
The poets and composers,
Study the songs, the lore,
The spiritual, the gospel,
Songs of the fields,
        of the spirit,
                of suffering,
                        of ecstasy.

Show us the creations
Of a thousand, thousand
Artists and artisans,
Craftsmen and smiths
And makers of beautiful things,
Known and unknown,
Praised or not.

Ancient men writing
Ancient prayers
On ancient paper
With ancient pens.
All of this beauty
Down through the ages.
And each of us
Must know of this,
Learn of this,
Be shown these things.

We have hunger
For these things.
No wisdom, no beauty
Should be denied us.
We are, each and all,
Born with the God given

Right of access
To the aesthetics
Of our people
Here on earth (and beyond).

And no child walking
(or even crawling on his hands)
Can be denied this right.
None are below this.
No one is too poor,
        degraded,
            downtrodden
To be denied
This right.

You may say –
We are starving
And hungry.
We could not
Put attention
On beauty.
Then feed us!
Give us clean water.
Then show us the art.

This is the aesthetic
Legacy of our people.
We have a sacred right
To know this legacy,
To learn this legacy
And to be part of
This legacy.

For this work,
This aesthetic, this beauty
Is the work of the spirit.

Louis A. Swartz

And if we walk this earth,
We are part
Of spirit kind.

And being so
We have the Divine Right
To know this magnificence,
To know of this beauty,
To know this aesthetic.
It is our Birth Right.

{ 5 }

Aesthetics

The strongest fabric in this universe is the fabric
of dreams. They are the sacred cloth of life. A man
doesn't lose his dreams. He may lose track of them.
Each individual soul has the native capacity to
create and achieve infinite dreams.

To Play Again

After her stroke, Alma's fingers seemed too weak
To play the Classical Spanish Guitar.
Her once lustrous world turned very bleak.
The stroke had left a painful, jagged scar.
Light drained from her life like a dying star.

Juan Carlos, her old teacher, kind and wise,
Came to see her early on a Sunday.
His sole purpose was to revitalize
This rare artist who thought she couldn't play,
To help her to begin again some way.

"Hija! Squeeze my hand as hard as you can!
Good! You are a lot stronger than you know!
I have a simple and workable plan.
Start out real easy and your strength will grow."
Touching the strings, her face began to glow.

Daddy and the Art

My Daddy was alone in his room.
He fell fast asleep while reading.
He'd study with the hope to illume*
Some part of the life he was leading.
And stop the spiritual bleeding.

Sunday, we were walking in the park.
He took my hand and held it quite hard.
"Son, I feel I'm whistling in the dark."
This startled me and caught me off guard.
I perceived he'd lost his self-regard.

Again, I found him asleep in his chair
Holding a pencil and drawing pad.
His art was strong, vibrant and fair.
I knew this was my actual Dad.
The best view inside him I'd ever had

For years I tried hard to rekindle
The magnificent spark I saw there.
Knew doing the art would make him well.
I attempted to make him aware
He had a special talent and flair.

I wasn't able to get him to see
How much his own creation could mean.
He did not hear me, he was lost at sea.
I wasn't able to intervene.
He was gone in a way I'd not foreseen.

One spring day I brought him home a book,
The paintings of the Impressionists.
I asked him courteously to look.
The image of his face still persists,
His utter joy seeing these artists.

Illume—enlighten someone's mind
Urban Dictionary

Louis A. Swartz

Creations

I want to celebrate small personal creations.
A breakfast table set with garden flowers.
An old love letter from Grandma to Grandpa.
A child's painting of frogs and mice and snakes.
A party dress made with Mom's own hands.
Preserves in Mason Jars from wild blueberries.
Homemade bread fresh and warm from the oven.
Hand embroidered table cloth lain for special meal.

A house cleaned in every cubby and corner.
A kindness appropriately acknowledged.
A good deed performed in secret anonymously.
The tired stories of an old man really listened to.
Picking wildflowers in springtime with your daughter.
And infinite other creations infused with spirit.
These little creations are ultimately the soul of life.

Notes on Beethoven's Violin Concerto in D Major

The almost painful sweetness of
this music, nearly illimitable*
tenderness, almost inexpressible
in an earthly context.
To be able to communicate this:
a magnitude of tenderness not
known here on Earth, a concentration
of pure beauty, a willingness,
an ability, an intention
to communicate beauty of this
magnitude elicits supreme awe.

This is monumental
tenderness.
If he had come here and just
left this and then had gone,
it would have been
enough for any man.
Bless him eternally for having
communicated such
unrestrained grandeur.

You can walk forward into
the future having heard
this music, this message
of reverent compassion
and kindness. With it you can
confront anything – any
trial, any loss, any fortune.
For this is a special point of view
that you hold in your heart
for eternity and walk forward
with as a spirit.

Just to know that such
beauty exists and has been
written permanently
lifts the heart in all things.
Having listened to this
concerto and having understood
at least some of what was
imparted brings a limitless
spiritual joy that
will remain
forever.

*Illimitable—incapable of being limited or bounded
Macmillan Dictionary for Students

Circus Note

One of her sisters was
A tightrope walker.
One was a clown
And one a contortionist.
She, herself, wrote songs
And lived a life
Of dreams and magic.

Passion

To awaken in the early morn
With a thunder breaking in your soul.
See with the fresh eyes of a newborn.
Blue sparks flashing in the predawn gloom.
Morning sky filled with unfinished dreams.
Muses are crowding into my bedroom.
Painting a new world through sleepy eyes.
Thrilled once again to see life resume,
Coaxing yet another sun to rise.

Art

When I was very young
I could feel art.
I was struck by wonder
At every turn.
One fall morning
A thousand birds
Flying south,
I felt their beauty
Somehow in me.

Grandma knitting
Yarn of red and blue,
Green and yellow
Into a warm afghan
Under which we curled
On cold nights in winter.

Mommy in the kitchen,
Dusk light through window,
Baking fresh bread
For family dinner.
So lovely she was.

Aesthetic Remembrance

Early morning music,
A sweetness almost beyond
Human comprehension,
But not completely.

A remembrance, an intimation,
Something from another world,
Something long ago, ancient,
But not actually, not really.

Apparently beyond my grasp.
Its content and substance
Appears to be just beneath my awareness,
But not beyond my understanding.

Seeming unimaginable
As if it is to me unknowable.
Too perfect, too enormous to know
But not so far beyond me at all.

Believing it belongs to another place
To which I cannot gain ingress.
A sacred place I could not enter,
But not, in truth, denied me.

A world too holy for earthly me.
A beauty I'm unable to fully see.
Someone else's eternity.
But not really lost to me.

It isn't something that's not of me.
It's part of my spiritual memory.
The aesthetic of personal immortality.
The very fabric of ultimate destiny.

Louis A. Swartz

Dreams

The strongest fabric in this universe is the fabric of dreams.
They are the sacred cloth of life. A man doesn't lose his dreams.
He may lose track of them. Each individual soul has the native
capacity to create and achieve infinite dreams.

Old woman speaking to me
In a bar on 9th Avenue,
"I want to be a ballerina
And dance on the concert
stages of Europe."

Wrapped in a many colored shawl
Passed down through generations,
Tapping her clunky, old lady shoe
To the sound of the music in her mind.

"I want to dance the concert stages of Europe!"
She spoke with righteous and earnest intensity.
Just need a few weeks practice at the ballet bar.
I knew how to dance like a bird can fly."

"But if it doesn't occur and I don't perform
You can still always come by my kitchen
And I'll cook for you a tuna casserole
That is fit for the Lord of the Angels."

The Old Place

The aesthetic integrity
Of things, actual things—
A wooden sled with metal
Runners used winter after
Winter by generations of
Children – the old surface,
Smooth and shiny with wear.
Its grain exquisitely
Raised to fine polish.

A green-painted swing
That had been
In the backyard
Of the old house for a
Couple of hundred years.
Standing beside it.
Still imbued with the sweet
Semblance of dozens of lovers
Who had used this swing down
Through the many years
As a place to fall in love.

Wooden bowl and wooden
Spoon that had always been
Used to beat the eggs, stir
The batter. The grooves in
The bowl cut by the friction
Of a thousand, thousand stirrings.

Daddy's marvelous pen
With which he constantly
Wrote in his numerous notebooks:
His thoughts, his impressions,

The worlds he knew, those
Whom he loved, the things
Of his life and the wonder
He experienced from just
Living one more day.
His poems and paintings,
All of it was in there—
Silly, sacred and sublime
In his beloved notebooks.

The stain glass transom*
Over the entrance to
Grandma and grandpa's
House. Tiny pieces of
Multicolored glass painstakingly
Molded together by patient hands.

Birds and flowers etched
In the glass of auburn,
Lilac and blue lavender,
Dozens of reds and oranges
And every imaginable green.
That transom was always
A world in itself especially
At 5 o'clock in the afternoon
When the sun began to fall
In winter between the two
Houses across the street,
Horizontal light directly
Hitting the willing glass,
Creating an unrestrained
Spectrum of color.

Uncle Max's tobacco fragrance
Filling the house. I couldn't help

But celebrate the immense
Pleasure he received from that
Cigar.

There was an oak tree on
A hill above the old house.
Worn but still very much alive
In the places it had been rested
Upon through time. This tree was
A place cherished and
Nearly eternal.

Give me actual things
Made by man and gods
That hold life in them:

The wicker picnic basket
That had carried so many
Joyous meals. The old
Blue wheel barrow in the
Garden and the ancient
Watering can beside it.
The wooden trellis covered
With a thousand climbing roses.
The hidden trail far
To the back of the garden that
Lead to a sun-lit corner
Adorned with every conceivable
Color of Iris. There I would sit
By myself on a wooden
Bench and wonder and watch.
These things were real
To me as I grew.

Transom—A window above a door
Merriam Webster

Locket

This locket,
Kept for you
Knowing you
Would come back
Someday.
Stuff of dreams,
Imagination,
Creatures
Of dreams,
Creatures of
Imagination.
Kept it for you
In a holy place.
These dreams
Were made of
Sacred stuff,
The real stuff,
The stuff
That matters,
Stuff of
Imagination.

Give Me Living Things

Give me things passed
Down through generations,
Worn and used.
Things that absorb life
Year by year
And exude it:

The rocking horse
That Daddy made
With wood and leather.

Ancient house on the hill,
Green wooden shutters,
The temple garden.

Aged kitchen
With earthen oven,
Dried fruit and spices,
Smells of intoxicating
Fermentation,
Jars filled with wondrous
Substances utterly familiar
And completely foreign
In the same instant.

Give me living things.
Gather up the dust
The Angel left
Behind during her
Brief visit here.
Gather it and place
It in a sealed urn.

Give me love letters
Written in earnest
Generations ago.
These are the things
On which I live.

I pay tribute as well
To those who make these things.

They are the craftsman,
Sculptors and stone masons,
Painters and potters.

Give me things
Made by souls
With hands
And minds
For the joy of God
And Angels and mankind.

Give me Neapolitan Pizza
Made by hand
With unleavened dough
And spices handed down
Generation to generation.

Give me the gentle balm
Grandma made from forest things
That could draw away pain
And smelled like roses
And grapes and tree bark
All at the same time.

Give me made things
Filled with spiritual love,
Desire and passion,
Healing and beauty,
Wonder and usefulness.
Give me things
Into which the spirit
Is instilled.

We Can Hear the Music of the Angels

We can hear the music of the angels.
Podemos escuchar la musica de los angeles.

As I look out my window
At the Hollywood sign
Vast music of the city
Is gorgeously mine.

Sitting quietly still
At the window
I can discern a cello,
Melodic and mellow.

Beyond that, hearing a Latin sound
Woven into the fabric of night.
Seems like it rises from the very ground
Prompting folks to dance in the evening light.

The raucous, the boisterous, the sweet,
The soft, the raw, the light, the pretty,
Sound of saxophone and a drumbeat,
Music of this gracious, vibrant city.

Sweet sound of violin,
What I wouldn't give
To hear that melody again.

Music of ancient Asia,
Music of Appalachia,
Rock and roll,
Music of the soul
Rising from the holy hills.
Music I can hear
As I sit silent and still.

Louis A. Swartz

From window looking north
To the Hollywood Sign,
A world of music
For me and thee and thine.

Hold your breath,
Take in the city's
Length and breadth.
Music fills the world
Between birth and death.

Be still and hear
The music of the angels
La musica de los angeles.

The Iris Project

(This was written by a man who long ago made the flowers that we know today. He was a flower designer by inclination and trade. He participated in many projects, but his favorite by far was the assignment to design the Irises.)

Remember now a gentler
Time and a gentler place
Filled with special kindness
And a profound grace.
A magnificent light
Pervaded the space.
Recall those aesthetic hours
When we spent our time
Designing the flowers.

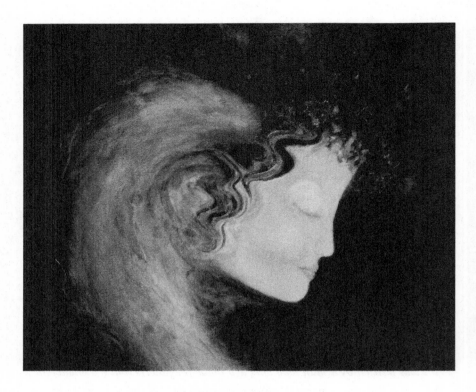

Visit from Iris

Visited last night by Iris,
Goddess of the Rainbow.
"To what do I owe this?"
In her blueberry eyes
I could see the sun rise.

"I have some colors want you to see."
She took me to her secret tower
Where she made colors by alchemy.*
In amazement, for the next hour,
I saw colors unknown here on earth
Made in her aesthetic laboratory.
Colors to which she'd just given birth.

She showed me a bright red, not just red,
But somehow at the same time was blue.
"This is for an angel's gown." she said
Then another color entirely new.

"How in the world do you do this?"

"I take the tears of a fair virgin
Who's never made love or yet been kissed
And in this liquid I mix therein
Sunspots and azure* drawn from the sea,
And some special stuff from Brooklyn
And create a color for eternity.
She left me with a marvelous vial
And said, "See you in a short while."

*Alchemy—any seemingly magical power or process of transforming
one thing into another
*Azure—clear sky-blue color
Macmillan Dictionary for Students

The Sketchbooks and Journals of a Flower Designer

(*Found in a cave near Toledo, Ohio, imprinted in the rock were tablets
of virtual electronic "writing" dating from hitherto unrecorded antiquity.
It was written in an ancient language that had been lost for eons. This was
finally transcribed from the rock and translated by the miracles of modern
technology.*

*They were discovered to be books of an early flower designer. They were
"written" and "drawn" on virtual "paper". Loosely translated, they had the
title of: "The Sketchbooks and Journals of a Flower Designer.")*

Notes from the first lecture of the Iris project

Most of you came from the Rose Designing Project. Beautiful job. Beautiful products.

The roses had their purpose and their singular beauty—the delicacies, subtleties, the rainbows of pinks. And then all the way to the depth of redness of the reddest red rose.

All of these creations are acknowledged, respected and venerated. They all have been carefully programmed into seed for future generations to adore. Thank you!

Now, we move to a different flower design project. The new flower begins at the apogee* of the Rose. This is a florid* flower to the nth degree. It is in your face, impudent, inexcusably beautiful, almost un-containable in an earthly context.

First of all, the very name of the flower is Iris, whom you all know well as The Goddess of the Rainbow. She will be working with us on this project as a consultant and she's just as excited about it as we are.

You have a very open palette with this one. Any color will go, any shade of any color. You can utterly splurge on color.

(A break here to see some initial Iris renderings.)

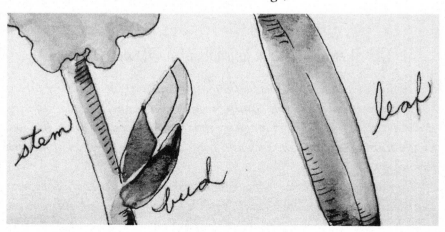

Lecture resumes

The basic design of the flower is quite specific. There will be six pedals on each blossom. Three of them will be upright and three of them will droop downwards. The leaves will be separate from the flower stem and shall be long, straight and sword shaped. More than one blossom can grow on an individual stem.

Personal notes in the journal of the flower designer.

I was one of the first guys to go on the Iris Project. Many things were tossed around in those early days. But as we worked and drew, a concept emerged. It would be a flower whose fundamental qualities were very different from the order and subtlety of the Rose.

This was a completely different concept. The idea here was an outrageous, unorthodox, disorderly, ordered flower, flamboyant,* unrestrained, seemingly out of control but as we worked turned out to be ingeniously controlled.

In the main, we weren't thinking in Rose type colors. We were working with deep purples and maroons and all manner of lavenders from pinky blues to blue blues and dozens of lovely purples.

There is something I wanted to note down here that is little known but extremely important. Before any of the flower designing projects began, there was a key idea put forward. This was the idea that something could exist *just to be beautiful*. Something for which there was no practical or logical reason.

This was the concept that there could be something in the universe *only* to be aesthetic, only to pervade loveliness. Amongst barren worlds this was an outrageously radical idea at the time. It was laughed at, made fun of, derided, ridiculed. It was asserted to be wasteful and superfluous (which is ironic because the word, superfluous has as its root *flo(u)r* meaning "blossom or finest part" and *super* meaning "over," "above" or "beyond." So it seems like superfluous means "having a great deal of the best of everything").

But even more importantly, ancient legend told us that *we were beauty* and that beauty was the finest thing there is in us.

So the Flower Project as it came to be known from its inception, was a project to design, create and then program into seed and thus bring into the world and propagate* this thing that had not existed before, this thing that had only one impractical, even illogical, reason for existence—to be beautiful. This was the flower, the purpose of which was and is to send out beauty, to embody beauty. Then through the miracle of the seed and the bulb, to send into the future that beauty for perpetuity.*

So there was a battle between two factions, one with the viewpoint that the design and creation of flowers was an unnecessary wasteful distraction and the other with the viewpoint that the creation and continuance of this beauty was vital to the existence of man.

Needless to say, we won! Just look at your garden or at the profusion of wild flowers blossoming on the hillsides in the spring and our victory will be visible.

*Apogee— the highest or furthest point
*Florid—highly decorated; gaudy; showy; ornate
Webster's New World College Dictionary.
*Flamboyant—...marked by elaborate, ostentatious or audacious display; Richly or brightly colored
American Heritage Dictionary
*Propagate—to grow new plants from seeds or from pieces cut from an existing plant or to make a plant produce more plants.
*Perpetuity—endless or indefinitely long duration or existence; eternity
Dictionary. com

Cello

(In acknowledgement of Vivaldi's Concerto for Two Cellos in G minor and Franz Josef Haydon's Cello Concerto #1)

Sound of the lone cello
Profoundly resonant
Touches the human soul,
Gracious and eloquent.
Awakens a world.
Hopeful message sent
Gentle yet vibrant,
Utterly resplendent,*
Echo of the soul,
Fully transcendent.*

*Vibrant—full of life, energy; resounding, resonant
Macmillan Dictionary for Students
*Resplendent—having a very bright or beautiful appearance
Cambridge Online Dictionary
*Transcendent—beyond or above the range of normal or merely physical human experience
Oxford Dictionary Online

Cello Again

"(Music) has the power of making heaven descend to earth."
— Japanese proverb

Summer's early morning rising sun.
Summer wheat russet,* gold and yellow.
Distant, but clear, through an open window,
Deeply received sound of the cello.

Spoke of something I am waiting for.
Music came from above to below.
Opened my world, opened a door.
Music from somewhere very long ago.
Loved ones and friends fondly remembered.
Truths and answers have great need to know.
Resonance of graceful cello's sound
Touched a chord way inside of me.
A lost world is now newly found.
Brief glimpse of what I need to see.
Warm and wondrous cello music
Heralding aesthetic destiny.

*Russet—reddish brown color
Macmillan Dictionary for Students

Louis A. Swartz

Memory of a Melody

Claire awakened to the warm morning sun
With a memory of a melody.
She was cooking breakfast for her grandson.
She heard music of human dignity.
Containing an astounding harmony.

She sat down at the table as he ate.
She had a joy she just couldn't express.
In awe, she was able to duplicate
A magnitude of profound loveliness
Which she was barely able to possess.

"This is a wonderful world, child!"
She told him while she helped him to dress.
The boy somehow understood and smiled.
"You are off to school. Goodbye and God bless."

She ran to the piano to write the score.
Unearthly melody she could now hear,
Something never faintly approached before.
The sound she heard was astoundingly clear.
She replicated the exquisiteness
Of this sound she was able to access.
Experienced unrestrained happiness.

Claire at the Piano

At dawn, Claire at the piano alone
Played a faintly remembered reprise,
Something, somehow, somewhere barely known.
A tune she could almost recognize.
Music so loving and genuine,
Beyond the human, touched the divine.

What really happens when a person dies?
The music appeared to speak to this.
There was something special to realize.
Engendered immeasurable bliss.
An idea of what living could be.
A small inkling of infinity.

Miss Helen Hilliard

Miss Hilliard taught me English in tenth grade.
She helped me understand I had value
And enabled me to be unafraid
To communicate the stark truths I knew.
In her classes she awakened and stirred
A love inside me for the written word.

{ 6 }

Ideas, Images, and Places

Living is the finest art.

Songbird

An urgent feeling there is something
Important I'm supposed to realize.
There's a songbird with a broken wing.
A hope so crucial to actualize.
The sun is rising in the eastern skies.

It's about my place in eternity.
The injured songbird still sings at sunrise.
I'm responsible for my history.
Understandings begin to crystallize.
The sun is rising in the eastern skies.

The angel is easy to recognize.
There is an openhanded* future
We can perceive in her kindly eyes,
Thoughtfulness she's come here to nurture.
The sun is rising in the eastern skies.

The songbird sings his joyful heart out.
The guarding angel, humane and wise,
Imbues* amazement in me throughout,
Causes an ancient purpose to arise.
The sun is rising in the eastern skies.

*Openhanded—liberal in giving; generous
Macmillan Dictionary for Students
*Imbue—to inspire or influence thoroughly
American Heritage Dictionary

In the Garden Remembering

The old man constantly
Walked down to the garden
Near the roses quietly
Remembering Brooklyn
And before that Berlin.

It was mainly the children,
Long since fully grown,
Recalled just as they were then,
Sitting outside the brownstone.
The cherished folks he'd known.

Dogwood petals floated
In the soft, warm spring air.
Robin sang sweet throated.
Thinking of songs and Claire,
He whispered a short prayer.

Bless his Heart

*Dedicated to my friend Bruce on the occasion of his receiving
a new heart in a heart transplant.*

He's here to help all he can.
He's always had so much heart.
Understand help, know the man.
Living is the finest art.

This soul needs a full lifespan.
He needs a good working heart.
We must bless this helping man.
Living is the finest art.

And bless as well his new heart.
May the heart be strong and fine.
A new chance to do his part
And give lots of helping time.
Living is the finest art.

Listen

The old man wants to get
Some things off his chest.
The child saw something beautiful
And wants to tell you about it.
Listen closely.

Someone is playing
A flute in a window
High above the street.
Listen closely.

Your wife had a thought,
She saw something.
She wishes to convey
Her admiration to you.
Listen closely.

Grandma has something
She needs you to hear
Before she travels on.
Listen closely.

Hear the creatures,
The big animals:
Scratching of the bear,
Quiet of the stalking tiger,
Trumpet of the elephant in love,
Whisper of the antelope passing.
Listen closely.

Know the sound of the sea birds
And the sea and its creatures,
The seagull and the albatross,

Louis A. Swartz

The voice of the whale
Not of this earth.
Listen closely

The villager tells tales
As night breaks over
The fields and huts.
Listen closely.

Be aware of the music of the masters,
Harmonic wisdom passed down,
A legacy from generation to generation.
Listen closely.

Perceive as well
The sound of the spirit,
Pervading kindness
Into the souls of men.
Listen beyond all
Imaginable listening.

Louis A. Swartz

Refugee

Riding top of the freight train
Under the vast desert sky,
An unforgiving terrain
Where it's so easy to die.

An utterly broken race,
Unspeakable disgrace
They have been coerced* to face.
Still retain their native grace.

Child vainly* searches for food.
Girls disguised to avoid rape.
Countless dangers to elude.
Necessity to escape.

The limitless dignity
Possessed by the refugee,
Passionate integrity.
Ask an end to enmity.*

Learn their stories, learn their names.
Respect their strength of courage
Which in spite of all remains.
They flee from a new dark age.

Their will to live keeps them sane.
As they cross a border again.
Maybe a place that's humane,
Where they can soften the pain.

Open your hearts.
Open your doors.
Open your homes.
Open your shores.

Perceive the humanity
Of these discarded people,
A part of conflict's debris,
War's uncalled for agony.

These people are so worthwhile.
They come here in honest flight,
Needing work, free from guile.
It's not hard to know what's right.

Lay you down your weary load.
Rest here with us a while.
The end of a tortured road,
You have now walked your last mile.

*Coerced—to force, as by physical violence, threats or authority
Macmillan Dictionary for Students
*Vainly—not successful or effective
Macmillan Dictionary for Students
*Enmity—the bitter attitude or feelings of an enemy or of mutual enemies; hostility; antagonism
Webster's New World College Dictionary

Matters

Each increment of help matters.
Each increment of compassion
And kindness matters.
It may be all that matters.

Louis A. Swartz

Those Summers When the Warm Wind
Blew East Across the Plain

Where the river
Subtly curved
Near the sand island,
Where the heron walked.
Warm summer
Wind blowing
Gently east
'Cross the plain,
Soft brown grass
On the hills.

Solitary
Standing oak
Deeply rooted,
Tenacious and
Nearly forever.

Returned there,
Late summer,
Just before
The first rain.
Returned there
With a hope
To perceive a trace
Of our lives
Together there.

Remembrance
Of the laughter
Shared together,
The wondrous
Stories told.

Those summers
When the warm
Wind blew east
Across the plain.

India

The elephant,
The child's hand,
The rhino walking,
Sandals by the door,
Child breast feeding,
Fresh fields following
The downpour,
Sweet smell of spices,
Dinner cooking
In the village,
Darkness falls,
Tiger walking.

Louis A. Swartz

Indian Nightfall

The tiger stirred in his sleep.
The elephant sighed
At the edge of the forest.

The Indian moon rose
Gorgeously over
The huts and houses
Of half a billion
Indian lovers,
Making love
Or making chai
Or somehow making do.

Enduring another
Night of hunger
Or watching movies
From Bollywood*
On flat screen TVs.

Hollow-eyed child
Sitting on his haunches
In the corner
Of the room
In a tiny village
In the Deccan*
Filled with wonder
And apprehension.

Mama nursing
New born daughter
Who drinks hungrily.
Mama hoping for
A kinder world for her.

Millions of bicycles
Resting for the night.

Hungry tiger wakens
And begins to paw
Through the night
In search of
Living sustenance.

Two elephants
Make love thunderously
Beside a quiet
Pool of water.

Restless nightfall
Of Mother India.
May the gods
Bless the people.

*Bollywood—Refers to the film industry of India, a play on "Hollywood"
*Deccan—a hot dry plateau in south, central India

Amnesty

An open poem written to those who have grievously harmed their
fellow man or who have committed crimes against humanity.

Definitions:

*Amnesty – noun – general pardon, especially as given by a government
to prisoners, outlaws, or rebels. [Modern Latin: amnesia from Greek am-
nessia forgetfulness, supposedly with reference to a Greek general's offering to
forget the wrongs done by his enemies]– Macmillan Dictionary for Students*
*Pardon – verb trans. – 1. To release (a person) from punishment for an
offense*
*2. To pass over (an offence) without exacting penalty or placing blame;
forgive [Old French: pardoner to forgive, done, bestow from Late Latin par-
donare to remit, give wholeheartedly from Latin per thought + donare to give]*

*I realize that the poem below will probably be considered controversial.
There are those who require amnesty because they have been legitimately
persecuted. But there are others who seek amnesty as a way to hide from
their crimes.*

*The practical implementation of an amnesty program would have to
include a real look at who could be able to participate in such a program.
There have been individuals who have committed crimes against humanity
of such magnitude that it calls into question the value of effort expended to
attempt to rehabilitate them. When there is also a complete lack of remorse
for these crimes, rehabilitation becomes nearly impossible.*

*However, when the individual is willing to publicly communicate in
writing all of his crimes and harmful acts, willing to do honest restitution
for his acts no matter what it takes, then, in my view, there could be a
possibility for amnesty.*

*This is an idea for a hoped for more benevolent future time when the jus-
tice system may move more in the direction of rehabilitation than retribution.*

With such crimes you ask for safe passage?
You hear those cries of utter outrage?
Dare you to ask for sanctuary?
You plead to avoid the hanging tree?
Your own right to life is self-bestowed.
The first step is to pay all debts owed.

We're unable to provide you peace
And to cause your misery to cease.
Now, I can show you where you can start,
But I can't cause calmness in your heart.
I'm not able to give you peace of mind
Or understanding from humankind.

With gross crimes against humanity,
A man can't get off that easily.
Atrocities we cannot believe.
Relief for the soul is self-achieved.
You confront your evil's length and breadth.
Responsibility ends not with death.

This concerns destruction of nations,
Forget your false justifications.
The ice you are walking on is thin.
This is the place you can now begin
To be of these gruesome horrors free.
The first step is take the amnesty.

Your crimes have caused their personal toll.
You can reverse the death of your soul.
We give no promise or guarantee.
Just honestly take the amnesty.
The next step you come utterly clean.
Confront what you've done and who you've been.

Next, make a plan of restitution.*
This needs to be your own solution,

Louis A. Swartz

Your own personal contribution.
You need to be honest and forthright.
You yourself can make it be all right.
This is not just accomplished overnight.

We don't desire retribution.*
You figure out the restitution.
You need not live with your crimes and lies,
Honest, fair justice can be realized.
You can change your perverse destiny
And can return to humanity.

*Restitution—the act of making good or compensating for loss, damage or injury
American Heritage Dictionary
*Retribution—punishment for the evil done
Webster's New World College Dictionary

So Many Have Given So Much

So many have given so much.
Weren't in it for themselves as such.
It was a very different age,
When we started on this voyage.
There was so much we didn't know.
So much bigness in which to grow.

It's coming to work day by day
And sticking with it come what may.
Learning the lessons page by page.
Growing wiser while we age.
Creating enormous *espirit*.
That's exactly what it's meant to me.

For all those here from near the start,
Who worked so long and played their part,
Each increment of help mattered.
For them, duty was their guideword.
Their early contribution was key
To our ultimate victory.

Help

We are natively openhearted
Helpers of our fellows.
We are joy.
We are beauty.
We are help.

Laughing Man

Laughing man,
His great and
Mirthful soul
In his eyes.
Complete in himself
He did not
Realize
How singularly
Beautiful
And wise
He was.

When All is Said and Done

When all is said and done
As we each move on,
As we strike our tents
And take our leave again,
There remains ultimately
This and this only:
The decency practiced,
The kindness purveyed,*
The help rendered* and received.

*Purvey—to furnish or supply
*Render—to give; deliver
Webster's New World College Dictionary

Death, the Spirit, and Immortality

Any way you cut it, death is wicked rough.

If you're going to be immortal, you must have something for which to live.

I see the world through eternal eyes.

Death can kiss my kosher rear end.

Louis A. Swartz

You Are Going to Get Well!

David, five years old, was extremely ill.
At bedside, in attendance, was Claire.
Light shone through flowers on windowsill.
She choked a hopeless thought in midair
And willed away her grief and despair.

"Listen kid! You're going to get well!"
Whispered as he slept to the young guy.
"Swift healing I'm able to foretell.
Need a miracle! Rough, but I can try.
I'm plain unwilling to let you die."

"I was looking for some kind of sign.
The doctors had long since called it quits.
It's beyond human, needs the divine.
This is now a job for the spirits.
It's now time I tested my limits."

I took his small hand and placed it in mine.
"Son, I ask you to come alive, now!"
I sensed something in me that was divine.
Knew I could reach him somehow.
Some way he told me, "Don't worry I'm fine."

A while later he opened his eyes.
"Oh Mommy, I wonder where I've been."
I could hardly hear through my heaving sighs.
Color rose in his face as I'd foreseen.
We were surrounded by strength unseen.

Springtime Walking Home

Walking home by myself in early spring,
Sun behind the trees in late afternoon.
Through a window sound of guitar string,
Resonant, solitary, a warm tune.
Possibly a sea change* is coming soon.

Later a schoolgirl waiting for the bus,
Her bright, clean face filled full with happiness.
Is there something she is imparting to us?
Although earth seems to grow more soulless,
She gave me a joy I cannot express.

An old man's greeting, solemn and friendly,
Transient and forever at the same time,
Sitting alone beneath the maple tree,
Listening to the bells of Saint John's chime.
How on earth could anyone be so sublime?

Reaching our home, at the piano was Claire.
Last light of sunset through the high window.
The music appeared to voice a prayer,
Telling me there's something I need to know.
Saw a good future in the afterglow.

Sea change—a transformation, esp. a major one
Webster's New World College Dictionary

Louis A. Swartz

Geezers*

In the San Francisco sunrise,
Two frail old men sat on a bench
Speaking Yiddish I recognized.
"Listen Issac, act like a mensch!*"
Laughing 'til tears came from their eyes.
Cared not about their age or ills.
One more time to sit with your friend
As the sun rose above the hills.
They didn't agree life had an end,
"Death can kiss my kosher rear end!"
Joy of living fully awakened.

*Geezer—An old person, especially an eccentric old man
*Mensch—a person of integrity and honor [Yiddish, human being]
American Heritage Dictionary

If You're Going to be Immortal, You Must Have Something for Which to Live.

Margaret sat by the window
Watching the children play
In the street down below.
They were shouting and laughing.
She couldn't get into the spirit.
She turned to the TV and idly
Watched and turned away.
"I would read a book,
But my eyes are going."

She went over again in her mind
The day George left her in 1967.
"I thought I was a good wife.
I had gained a lot of weight.
We stopped talking to each other.
He stayed out to all hours of the night.
He grew increasingly morose.
The life went out of the marriage.
There was no joy in it at all."

The Ice Cream Man arrived.
Ringing his bell alerting the children
There were sweet ice cream cones.
Children swirling around the truck.
"I wish I could be excited like that."
The sun was setting behind the fire escape.
"I used to love this time of day, so serene.
If I could have that feeling again,
I would surely give all I have."

Louis A. Swartz

"If I could be again the woman I once was...
I was so beautiful as a young girl.
The boys whistled at me in the street.
I played the violin like an angel.
I could draw perfectly any face I saw.
I had dreams, oh I had dreams.
Brooklyn was thrilling to me then.
Each day was an unbroken adventure.
What has become of me now?"

"I have become a bitter old woman.
I have lost touch with my aesthetic.
I detest being a fat shapeless lump.
I have grown old against my will.
I cannot walk a flight of stairs
Without gasping for breath.
My legs strain to support me.
If I could return to a trace of myself,
If I could recover a tiny piece of me...

"How do I get back to that romance?
Do I place a personal ad on line?
'Old lady, 73, five feet two inches,
87 pounds overweight, seeks lover'
Don't think I'd get much response.
But maybe there's another way.
I think my drawing pencils
Are in the basement with my violin."

She went down to the musty basement.
Beneath a plastic Christmas tree almost
Crushed she found her violin. Under stacks
Of women's magazines she found her drawing
Pad and pencils. She sat on the basement floor
Cleaning the violin. She tightened and plucked

The strings. She felt a long forgotten surge rise.
"Can I still play?" She opened the drawing pad,
Leafed through some of her old drawings,
"My God I was good!"

Later, upstairs, drawing pencil in hand, she
Drew the children playing in the street below.
As she drew she felt a feeling of personal pride
She had not felt in forty years.

Louis A. Swartz

Eulogy

To Megan

A few weeks ago I lost you.
That's not the right word.
There is a much truer way
To describe this experience.
I have not the perception
To be able to follow you
In this transition.
I do not mourn a loss.
I protest an interruption.

Just a few weeks ago
You exuberantly spoke
Of your beloved son.
You had expansive plans,
The mutual adventures
You hoped to experience
With your son as he grew.
I protest this specific joy
Is not available to you.

And that you were required
To leave so suddenly.
However, you are not gone.
You are still you.
You will be able to see
All your long term dreams
Through to full accomplishment.
You perceive life now
From a different viewpoint.

Every increment of help
That you rendered matters.

The succor you provided
To so many helped so much.
The loveliness you imbue
Into the world is so appreciated.

All these things are not
Of the fleshly or physical.
These are the qualities
That belong to the spirit.
We bless your passage
From one viewpoint
To the next viewpoint.
There will be others there
To help and to heal.

The Last Letter Written by the Old Man Before He Died

Dearest Jeannette,
 I was profoundly moved by your letter.
 Please forgive the inordinate
amount of time it has taken
me to answer you. My only
feeble, but true, "excuse"
for my tardiness is that you
gave me so much to contemplate,
it has taken me this long
to assimilate it and return
the communication to you.
 First of all, what you
Said about your perception of
grace in each individual
person moved me more
deeply than I can easily say.
 The story of that old man
who you saw every morning in
the park sitting on that
bench between the lilies
and the climbing roses in
his old, worn woolen coat
even in the height of summer,
touched something huge inside
of me. How he would smile at
you each morning with what
utter joy in his face and how
you could directly perceive
his spirit (or him somehow)
beyond his deeply wrinkled
face, beyond his gnarled
hands and old cracked

finger nails, there was a
life that danced around
him and through him and
sent sparks out of his eyes
—something holy, something
sacred, something somehow
forever.
    As well, the love you felt
for him. I understand that
so well. I have experienced
love like that, transcendent,
reaching into the future,
reaching into always and
ever. His face as you saw
it, old though it was against
the blue, purple lavender of
the lilacs. His face, old as sin
and yet with laughing eyes
against these lilacs
powerfully alive just like them
and yet, simultaneously
about to transform.
    A face looking into the
future in almost the same
way the face of a very
pregnant mother configures
or seems to configure
into two faces. The face of
now and the face of the
future. I shared the perception
with you as I too have seen
this and it has taken my
breath away.
    Benny came by yesterday.

He brought some pickled
herring. We ate it together.
It was delicious. He told
me he had fallen in love,
but didn't want to get into it.

Meg came by to check
on me. She is such a delight.

I noticed the first signs of
fall this morning, a few
scattered red leaves on the
maple.

I need to get moving. Please
give my love to everyone.

      Love,
      Dad

The Old Man's Death

My old man did not die easily,
Too much undone,
Too much regret,
Too much mystery.

An agitated death
Devoid* of quietude.*
I wanted to tell him,
"Daddy, this is not
The end of the road."
But he was already
Half into the next world
And could not hear me.

A tragic lack of education
On the nature of death.
It is not a pity that men die.
It is a pity that they know not
Where death will take them.

They face eternity or nothing
With a pervasive* hollowness
That does not relent
At the edge of death.

*Devoid—not possessing; lacking (with of)
Quietude—state or condition of calmness or tranquility
Macmillan Dictionary for Students
Pervasive—to spread throughout
Webster's New World College Dictionary

Louis A. Swartz

So Long Friend

Towards the end
You ascended*
Into a holiness
Difficult
To comprehend.
Each, perforce,* brief
Conversation
Valuable beyond belief.
Knew you'd be back
But wasn't letting go
Easily at all.
Anyway you cut it,
Death is wicked rough.

We are creatures
Who cherish the familiar,
The known touch,
Your touch, your voice.
Familiar footsteps
That have always
Preceded you
And remained as you
Took your leave.

However, good bye
Is utterly
Inappropriate.
So long, friend.

*Ascended—to go up; move upward; rise
*Perforce—by or through necessity
Webster's New World College Dictionary

By and By

As on the sea your ashes scatter,
Help you've rendered, gracious things you've done,
These are the things that really matter.
Upon death these things are not undone.

It is extremely easy to see
By your personal actions alone
You will determine your own destiny.
It's the person into whom you have grown.

It's you that lives on when you're gone,
The man you are, not your earth name,
With full awareness this carries on.
It's the inextinguishable flame.

It is who you are as a spirit
That determines your life after you die.
Things temporal* cause things infinite.
It is not needed to say goodbye.
This will become realer by and by.

*Temporal—of this world, worldly, not spiritual
Webster's New World College Dictionary

Louis A. Swartz

Childhood's Bed

Sitting alone in child's room
Expecting him to return soon.
Sitting there bleakly on his bed
Trying to fully remember
All the important things he said.
By myself there on childhood's bed.

Stacked up child's wooden blocks
Of purple, yellow, blue and red.
Confronting unthinkable loss
And utter emptiness ahead.
Trying some way to reach the boy.
Unable to believe he's dead.

Can hear through an open window
Somehow, "Daddy, I am still here.
I am with you. I did not go."
Just above me, a sweet song heard,
The green tree branches gently stirred,
Soothing melody of the Blue Bird.

San Francisco Early Morning

I awakened thinking of you.
As the wind picked up on the Bay,
The white sails of early sailboats
Gracefully leaned into the stiff breeze.
The fog lifted from the shoreline.

Spread on my desk near the window
Letters from you from so long ago,
Grainy photos of folks long gone.
I was rearranging my mind
To visions of a gentler time.

I looked out across the Golden Gate
To the lush blue green coast beyond.
A loss I couldn't ameliorate.
Wherever you are, I hope you're fine.
I wish to see you in a future time.

Passing

His eyes fluttered
And fluttered no more.
A great spirit
Filled the room with laughter.
Humbled and awestruck,
We went to prepare the wake.

Remembrance

He'd possessed a beauty I could see.
Open kindness was self-evident,
The utter joy of his company.
Did he know what his presence meant?
He's not here but he isn't absent.

Walking the August Beach

I was walking the August beach.
The things I am able to know.
The things I am willing to teach.
Sacred places I wish to go.
The world just beyond my reach.
Our joyous life lost in the breach.*

Death and sadness pervade my mind.
Memories wrenching and bittersweet.
Welcome the grace of humankind.
Acknowledgement of life complete.

Warm summer wind washes away
My loss, my sorrow, tears and grief.
Goodbye is not easy to say.
Song of the sea bird brings relief.
You will return some other day.

*Breach—state of being broken; a rupture; a break
Noah Webster's 1828 Dictionary

The Spirit's Name is Kindness

Configured* of wonderments,
Endowed with humor and grace,
Eloquence and astonishments.
Morning sun reflects in his face.
Surpassing joy he can express.
Know the spirit's name is kindness.

*Configured—to construct or arrange in a certain way
Webster's New World College Dictionary

Eternal Eyes

My son caught his breath
As the bells began to toll.
What're his thoughts on death?
Then came the drum roll.

Don't be sad my brave son.
The great man we now mourn
Was a phenomenon.
He didn't die. He is ever-born.

There are things we cannot see
But can perceive without eyes.
What's it take for a man to be free
And able to see another sunrise?

"Listen to me Dad. I understand.
This to me is not a surprise.
I have experienced it firsthand.
I see the world through eternal eyes."

Above All

Above all, it comes down to this.
These wildflowers covering
The steep hillside,
A concentration of color,
Bright, bright yellow
Intermingled with orangish
Yellow and reddish brown.
Springtime on the prairie.

Above all, it comes down to this.
The care of this wife.
The wonder of these children.
The value of dreams dreamt.
It comes down to the seasons,
The great snows to the west
In the mountains.
And finally spring again,
Remembering how much
This means to us.

Above all, it comes down to this.
The deer are now returning
From the warmer valleys below.
It is the constant and profound
Love I feel for my wife
And my children.
The spirit that engenders*
This intensity of life each spring.
It is enough to fully understand
One single flower blooming.

Above all, it comes down to this.
You needn't wait

Louis A. Swartz

For what you're expecting.
Eternity is woven
Into the fabric
Of everyday life.
All that is required
Of each individual man
Is to see the world
Which surrounds him.

Above all, it comes down to this.
It is here that the invisible
Meets the visible.
The colors of these myriad*
Wildflowers are the colors
Of the human soul.
You need not wait for answers.
Your answers are in the living world
That you see before you
This very morning.

Above all, it comes down to this.
Look through to the perfection
Of each living thing.
The first new green leaves opening.
Each living soul
Has a right to witness
This eternal life.

*Engender—to bring into being; bring about; cause; produce
*Myriad—a great number of persons or things
Webster's New World College Dictionary

Destiny

You can't degrade or damage your fellows
Without grave eternal consequences.
You will determine the way the wind blows.
You practice evil at your own expense.
What you create decides your recompense.*

If you're immortal you need to contend
With your own self and deeds for eternity.
Plain to see what the future will portend.*
You cause the glory and catastrophe,
The actual nature of your destiny.

*Recompense—reward
Webster's New World College Dictionary
*Portend—be a warning sign or indication of
Macmillan Dictionary for Students

Joy for the Long Run

There is nothing more beautiful
Than the native divinity
Of a spirit alive in full,
Fulfilling his own destiny.

Able to have outrageous fun,
Living's magical harmony.
Unrestrained joy for the long run.
Glimpse of what it is to be free.

Turn into a Skylark

Jump off the treadmill
With fierce laughter
In your eyes.
Change your shape.
Perhaps turn
Into a Skylark
Or an Arctic Tern
And fly vast distances
Over oceans and land.

Insights

A sense of pride in the divine within me,
Gaining touch with myself as a spirit.
Immortality's possibility.

Grand and new thoughts stayed with me overnight.
The morning city was warmed with sunlight.
A universe opened with this insight.

Glimpse of a Universe Unseen

Awe inspiring creations I've seen,
The truths I've been able to learn and know
Are a glimpse of a universe unseen.
Profound emotion felt from long, long ago,
This almost uncontainable rapture
Expresses life's unacknowledged grandeur.

One's capacity for astonishment,
Our own ability to be amazed
Provide the necessary nourishment
By which the human spirit can be raised
To approach his native magnificence,
Manifest his inborn beneficence.*

There are children faraway ice skating
Beneath lightly falling powdery snow.
It's as if a new world is waiting.
Children's laughter echoes up from below.
Seeing the world with different eyes.
So much to learn. So much to realize.

*Beneficence—the practice of doing good; active goodness, kindness
Noah Webster's 1828 Dictionary

Louis A. Swartz

Fresh Water Spring

I am now remembering things
I have known for a thousand years.
It was at this turn in the trail
Where the sun still suffuses*
Through the oak branches
As it has for a thousand years.

The rock face above is still warmed
By the sun in the early morning
As it has been as long as time.

In the fall the big birds soar south
Kept aloft by the warm wind
Rising from the valley floor.

They have rested by the river
On the soft fallen leaves
Since before the Yuki Indians
Came to the river to settle.
In the morning, with the sun,
They take off again for the south.

There was a fresh water spring
Here a thousand years ago.
Deer gathered at the pond below.
Wild roses grew in profusion here.
Yes! I see the spring I remembered!
As it has been for nearly forever.

Below the rock shelf, cool and moist,
Grow forest ferns silent and joyous.
I am happy here on this earth
Having come here again and again.

I have walked these trails
And tasted this pure spring water.

The deer have come close unafraid.
I think they want to study me.
Big birds fly high above us.
The wild roses, solitary for ages,
Are joyed to have someone see them,
To have the pleasure of their fragrance.

*Suffuse—to spread through or over, as with light, color, or emotion Macmillan Dictionary for Students

I Had Not Expected You

I had not expected you.
The sun was setting
Behind the yellowish hills
Of late summer in Sonoma.

I was busy with daily life,
Caring for the children,
Tending to the apple orchard,
Pruning the apple branches.

Getting on with the work
Of the living.
In the kitchen making dinner.
Sewing holes in boy's pants.

I had not expected you,
But it was a joy to perceive you
As children played by the pond below.
Could you smell the bread baking?

I always knew you were somewhere,
But it tickled me to no end
To have you sitting on my shoulder,
Just as silly as you'd always been.

Profusion* of Lilacs

In a corner of the garden
there was a profusion of lilacs,
intensely fragrant, a whole
world of blue and purple,
deep blue blue
to lavender blue,
to completely unapologetic
dark red royal purple
framed by uncompromising
giant, vibrant, fragrant
vital magenta trees.

It was there I most
profoundly perceived you
and where without words
we spoke. We walked
together (without legs)
through the stories of our lives.

*Profusion—rich or lavish supply; abundance
Webster's New World College Dictionary

Louis A. Swartz

New Jersey Shore

When all is finally said and done,
I'm still looking for something more.
As shadows lengthen in setting sun,
Know there's vast purpose to live for,
Green beach umbrella on Jersey Shore.

Remember the summers of childhood,
When I believed in forevermore.*
We would collect seashells and driftwood
In the early forties clothing we wore,
Green beach umbrella on Jersey Shore.

Another chance to create some good.
To be a young boy yet once again
On the late summer beach in Wildwood.
High overhead graceful seabirds soar,
Green beach umbrella on Jersey Shore.

*Forevermore—for eternity; for always
Collins On Line Dictionary

Our Time Here

Why, when this tenure
Here on earth,
Which seems
So transitory,
Why is there such
Intense value to it?

Why does each day
Matter so much?
Why does it seem
So imperative
That every day lived
Results in product?

Is there a higher purpose?
Is there a greater aesthetic
To which to strive?
Is there much more
To us than is visible?

Are we being prepared
For a greater mission?
Why does it seem
That each human contact
Matters so very much?

For what reason is it
That what we learn here
Has such enormous value?
It seems that how
We create our lives
Is of paramount importance.

Every interaction,
Every communication
Matters beyond belief.
There is absolutely
No room whatsoever
For a shoddy, insincere,
Wasted, mediocre life.

Somehow the stakes
Are much too high.
If there is a higher game
All of mankind
Needs to participate.

Each living day provides
Ample opportunity
To do good,
    listen,
       understand,
To help,
  imbue wonder,
      create beauty,
To raise up our fellows.

And somehow
Each increment
Of goodness
Put forth
Matters hugely.
The sum of these
Increments
Is the reason
We are here
And will continue
To be here.

Epilogue

It is the silences between words
I essay to somehow express.
I remember the special space
Between your two front teeth.

There was a palpable hollowness
In Grandma's room after she left
Consisting of the absence
Of all that she had been.

The breathing emptiness of rooms,
Bodies and lives no longer occupied.
Untellable awarenesses emerge
In the fertile interface* between
The mortal and the immortal.

*Interface—a surface forming a common boundary, as between bodies or regions
American Heritage Dictionary

Acknowledgements

I wish to say a word for my wife, Connie, who for the many years of our marriage, has given me constant support, encouragement and help. My editor, Patricia Ross, who has helped me immeasurably to make my writing understandable by my readers. My friend, Bernard Percy and his wife Caralyn who believe in me. My illustrator Diane Woods opened a whole visual world to me. I want to thank George Gluchowski, CEO Hugo House Publishers, for his unflagging support.

My thanks to Ronda Taylor, my designer, who so beautifully presents the work. Appreciation to Tom Solari and Randall Michael Tobin for their artistic understanding of what I am intending to accomplish. Thank you James and Kate Mumma for your support.

Once again, to Janadair for her perfect calligraphy, well done. Thank you Ingrid Gudenas for helping me in ways too numerous to detail here. Also my thanks to Laura Betterly for her help in marketing. Thanks to Nan Soler who helped me get started on getting my poetry out into the world. My gratitude to Stan Dubin who has helped me all along with wisdom, guidance and encouragement. I want to validate Colin Swartz and Becca Thompson who helped with key areas on how to present the book.

Again, to my 10th grade English teacher, Helen Hilliard, who brought out the magnificence in me. I wanted to acknowledge who I consider to be the poets of my generation: Bob Dylan, Paul Simon, Neil Young, Paul McCartney and many others for their inspiration.

Finally, I wanted to mention the German Poet, Rainer Maria Rilke, from whom I first learned that you can and must communicate about the most profoundly felt beliefs and perceptions.

A Note from the Author

Thank you very much for reading *Magic Realized*. I am very interested in your thoughts, perceptions, ideas, viewpoints and feelings on the book. I would love to hear from you. Please write to me via my publisher at the following addresses:

Email: George@HugoHousePublishers.com
(Please write in the Subject box, "A message for Louis Swartz")

Mailing Address:
Louis A. Swartz
c/o Hugo House Publishers, Ltd.
8816A Clearbrook Trail
Austin, TX 78729

Magic Realized is a book in its own right and can be read by itself. It is also volume 2 of a Series entitled *Constructed of Magic*. The first volume of the series, *Constructed of Magic* is available and is, in my view, a complement to *Magic Realized*. Below is how to order *Constructed of Magic*.

Hugo House Bookstore:
https://hugohousepublishers.com/product/
constructed-of-magic-paperback/

Amazon (Kindle), **Barnes & Noble** (NOOK)
and many other fine retailers across the globe.